Do you Have the Courage to Be You?

YOU WERE CREATED ON PURPOSE FOR A PURPOSE

DO YOU HAVE THE COURAGE TO BE YOU?

YOU WERE CREATED ON
PURPOSE FOR A PURPOSE

JENNY WILLIAMSON

NEXT CENTURY
PUBLISHING

Do You Have the Courage to Be You?

Published by Next Century Publishing
www.NextCenturyPublishing.com

ISBN: 978-162-9038339

Printed in the United States of America

DEDICATION

To my husband Mike and our sons, Austin, Michael-Dean and Ben.

I love you madly. I would give my life, my time, and, my last dime for you. My longing to matter in this world has never diminished my role as your wife and mother. Thank you for letting me take this journey of purpose. I know you have not always understood it. However, none of you ever asked me to stop. If you had, I would have said yes.

I pray you each find what I have—the courage to be and do all God created you to, nothing more, but absolutely refusing to settle for less.

You are each water walkers, giant slayers, and history makers.

Always do what you love to do—the thing that makes your heart sing—and you will change this world.

DO YOU HAVE THE COURAGE TO BE YOU?

YOU WERE CREATED ON
PURPOSE FOR A PURPOSE

CONTENTS

INTRODUCTION

You were created specifically on purpose for a purpose. Yes, you! I am talking about you.

Do you have any idea what your particular purpose is? Have you ever contemplated the fact that your destiny could change lives or even the world? Did you know there are people waiting for you to have the courage to be you?

Do not feel bad if your answer to these questions is *no*. You are not alone.

I have found that most people do not have a clue as to why they are on this planet. Thoughtfully planned, uniquely molded, and specifically created on purpose for a purpose sounds like a nice concept, and one much better than being a random cosmic accident. The trouble is, most of us have no idea how to find our specific purpose even if we believe we have one. We do not see much evidence in the people we know and love living courageous, purpose filled lives. That evidence we only seem to find in the movies we watch or the books we read. Heroes, we call them. Extraordinary individuals. We do not see or believe we too are essential, significant, or necessary to this world. Thus, we never go in search of who we truly are and what we were created to do. Sadly, settling for mediocrity and less than we were created for becomes our default mode. It just seems easier.

I understand.

I have felt pitifully ordinary for most of my life. I believed I had no particular recognizable talent that could be applauded by the masses. Talkative, hyperactive, loud, and bossy are not descriptions you list on a resume but are ones that were bestowed upon me. My career consisted of tasks that most anyone who had a high school diploma could have accomplished. Though being a mom to my boys is my most favorite thing in the entire world, they have all left home to begin their own lives. When they were younger and still at home, no one invited me to be on talk shows to discuss my extraordinary and world-changing parenting skills or provide a commentary on our afternoon at the park. I am not complaining. My life was good. It was just boring. I was cloaked in comfort and choking on mediocrity. I wanted to matter. I longed to make a real difference in this world, in my world. I wanted to believe there was a specific plan and purpose for *me*. So, near my fortieth birthday, I resolved to find it. Though it took some time, I did just that.

Now I want to help you do the same.

My journey of purpose and search for meaning has been an exciting one, but one that was more difficult and time consuming than I now believe was necessary. I wasted a lot of precious time asking the wrong questions and leaping in the wrong direction. I did most of it alone, blindly stumbling along an undefined path with no concrete *how-to's* or specific steps. It required a great deal of courage and faith to leave my comfort zones to travel into the unknown in search of my purpose. However, I would do it all over again. Every step was worth it. In the process, I have learned much that I love sharing with others. That is why I wrote this book – to save you time in discovering and beginning to fulfill your purpose. I believe the tangible, intentional steps I took and the lessons I learned will propel you quicker into your destiny. However, you must dedicate the time required and have the determination needed to make the courageous choices necessary to be and do all you were created to be and do. I will provide the encouragement and *how-to's*. I will be your coach and your cheerleader through the pages of this book and the words of my story.

I know my purpose is not your purpose; but through reading about mine, I believe you will see how God takes those of us who are convinced we are ordinary and does the extraordinary.

I will start at the end of my story.

We live in a world where children are sold for sex. It is wrong. More than wrong, it is horrendous, despicable, even loathsome.

When I first learned of this evil, I was sitting in church with two of my sons. My heart, my mother's heart, physically ached and I cried out loud for these faceless children. However, when I later learned it was also happening in my own backyard, I dried my tears and I got angry with God for this hideous injustice. I lashed out at Him and demanded *He do something!* Then deep within my heart, I heard Him quietly whisper to me:

Why don't you?

Because I am just a mom.

Good. That is exactly what these children need.

I do not have any money.

I will give you all you need.

People will think I am crazy.

So? These are your daughters, and your daughters are being raped, abused, tortured, and sold every single night. Why don't you do something?

Okay, but what?

Build them a home and call them family.

That sounded easy enough, so I did. And I am still doing this.

Since that day, my calling and my purpose have combined to become my life's work – rescuing girls who are being sold for sex, building homes around the world, and calling these girls "family." I am still ordinary and *just a mom*, but once I saw what was at stake, I was determined to *take courage* and be who I am so these kids would have the chance to be who they were created to be and do all they were created to do.

Which brings me back to you. I wonder who is waiting on *you* to be *you.*

When *you* have the courage to be *you*, lives are going to change! There will be more children rescued and restored; the hungry will be fed, the sick will be healed, the lonely befriended, and the brokenhearted comforted. There are people praying right now, waiting on God, and He is waiting on you.

Do you have the courage to be you, the *you* He created?

You do not have to be born courageous or feel brave; you just need to make daily choices that will move you into your water-walking, giant-slaying, history-making destiny. If you read this entire book and take the suggested steps, then you will be filled with a sense of urgency and boldness to do just that. You were created to be extraordinary. The world needs you!

Take courage!

Jenny Williamson

Do You Have the Courage to Be You?

There are two me's
inside of me.
The one I am.
And the one I long to be.
The one I am
is familiar and true.
She expects little of me,
yet dreams of more, too.
She seems somewhat less
while wanting something more.
But comfort surrounds her soul,
keeping her safe to the core.
Now the other ME that lives inside of me,
is the opposite for sure.
She plots and plans
her escape from the same.
She longs to do more,
to see more,
to be more,
all the while using my name!
The one me and the other
were once the same child.
But as time hurried onward
I lost her somehow.
I gradually began
wanting others to see,
just a mirror, a reflection
of themselves, instead of me.
I am not aware
when the thought first occurred.
Or when I recognized the truth,
But slowly I heard,
"How did this happen or come to be?
When did you become less,
so much less
than I designed you to be?"
At first I grew sad,
experienced a terrible ache.
I then began to ponder
all that was at stake.
Another thought surfaced,
as scary as the last,
what if others needed me to be me?

Then I better become me—fast!
A heavy sigh I let out,
as I began to pray.
"Lord grant me the courage,
(on this very day)
to cease to be
more of the same.
But for me to become me
and forever remain."
I then asked a question
of my Father so true,
"What does she look like—
this little girl I once knew?"
"Ah," He said,
"In her, I delight—
let me tell you her secrets
And how to give her life."
"She's as beautiful as a sunset.
An original of mine.
Man's approval does not matter,
as she completes her design.
She sings with the angels,
dances only for my smile.
Laughs with abandon,
knowing she is here for a short while."
"What are you afraid of?"
My Father asked of me.
"Don't you know by now
your purpose to be?
Lean close while I tell you
what you are longing to know.
I created you only; only so—
that you would be the me I designed you to be."
"Nothing more, my beloved one.
Settling for less cannot be done.
Take my hand and with courage soar
To the dreams and destiny
I have in store.
Safety and comfort are not yours to be
But a life lived fully alive so others can see
that they too were created for a great destiny."

PART ONE

Your Identity

CHAPTER 1

You Being You Matters

"Every man and woman is born into the world to do something unique and something distinctive and if he or she does not do it, it will never be done."

—Dr. Benjamin Mays

Before time began, you were imagined, planned, and lovingly created on purpose for a purpose—a specific, unique, and one-of-a-kind purpose for you and you alone. Deposited deep inside of you is everything you need to achieve your purpose in this life. Your purpose will transform lives and change the world. It is imperative that you succeed in discovering and fulfilling your destiny because lives are literally at stake!

I was shocked when I realized this truth applied to me.

"I would literally be dead if you had said 'No' to God. If you had quit, I would not be here. Thank you for rescuing me, for giving me a home and a family."

A twenty-three-year-old young woman said these words to me after her rescue from the world of sex trafficking. Her biological parents sold her to a man, a family friend, for the purpose of pornography, torture, and abusive sex when she was six years old. Trapped in slavery and owned by a series of men, she was trafficked around the world for the pleasure of one and the profit of another. When her hopes of rescue went unanswered, she began to pray that God would let her die. He did not honor this prayer. Despite her past and pain, He had good plans for her. Ones that involved my family and me. It was life changing to realize how much of an impact my life, my choices, and my purpose could have upon another individual.

Guess what? The Creator of the universe has life changing plans for you, too! Plans that affect you as well as others.

I am filled with such an urgency for you to believe this life-changing truth. When you are being you—the *you* God created you to be—lives *will be* changed, history *will be* made and prayers *will be* answered.

You Being You Matters

Have you ever contemplated your own uniqueness or dared to believe there is something distinctive that you alone were created to do, and if you do not dream it, create it, write it, tell it, sing it, or build it, *it* will not ever be done? Could history or lives really be at stake?

Yes!

Let yourself become pregnant with that possibility. Let these words sink deep within you to the place where your mind and logic cannot interrupt. Allow yourself the divine luxury of believing, for just a moment, that before time began, you were set apart for something great.

Before there was a moose or a mountaintop, before there was an ocean or an otter, a waterfall or walrus; before there were stars in the sky or lightning bugs in the dark, before there was a hippopotamus playing in the mud or a lion roaming the African plains, the Creator of the universe imagined you. He planned you and deliberately designed you for a specific, incredible, unique purpose.

Right here. Right now.

Imagine your Creator as a painter standing before an enormous blank canvas. You are the canvas. With meticulous strokes, He carefully considers the unique plans He has designed for you as He chooses your eye color, your personality, your IQ, and everything else about you. The sound of your laughter, the size of your feet, your aptitudes and abilities, as well as your weakness and vulnerabilities, are all part of your design with your distinct purpose in mind. The date and location of your birth was strategically determined to optimize your arrival and success. During your creative process, dreams and desires were deposited deep inside of you that, when activated, will lead you to your purpose and destiny.

The thought that went into creating you is inconceivable and mind-boggling.

All of creation is holding its breath in eager anticipation waiting for you to become you.

This fact should move you, expand you, and enlarge your view of yourself! Embrace the fact that you are truly one of a kind and not just a random accident. What has been planned for you, and only you, will astound you!

Created on Purpose

Dare to believe that before you were formed in your mother's womb, you were set apart for greatness. You playing *small* benefits no one. You being *less than you* accomplishes nothing. **You were created on purpose for a purpose.** Believe it! Allow that phrase to penetrate your heart. Shove aside your insecurities and embrace the fact that your Creator intends to display His splendor in you. To shine as bright as a star is your destiny.

These truths have transformed my life, and still propel me out of bed every morning. They override my insecurities and fears.

Although life altering and highly addictive, this journey of figuring out who you are and why you are here is not an easy one. Quite honestly, it is incredibly difficult and very scary because it forces us to leave our well-crafted comfort zones for the unknown, the secure for the insecure, and the possible for the impossible. It requires courage to be and do all we were created to.

For a long time, I believed courage was a personality trait—one I was *not* born with! I am not one to pursue adrenaline-producing adventures or activities, and I never feel the least bit deprived by that. I prefer activities that produce feelings of comfort, safety, and security. Sunday afternoon naps are high on that list, as is reading a good book by a warm fireplace, taking a hot bubble bath, and drinking a glass of California red wine made by a trusted and familiar winemaker. I like to go to the same places, eat the same foods, and hang out with the same people. I am an expert at avoiding surprises and anything that could possibly evoke fear or uncertainty, such as trading stocks, 100-percent-commission sales jobs, vacations with strangers, new restaurants, or starting a non-profit organization.

I want my feet to be on solid ground at all times, and I want to know *exactly* what is about to happen, at least five years in advance. As you can imagine, flying through the jungle on a zip line, bungee jumping off a bridge, or parachuting from a small twin-engine airplane are not on my bucket list, even though their instructors promise you are safe as they strap you in.

For those of you who do these things on a regular basis, you may find the journey to a courageous, purpose-filled life an easy one. The rest of us, who are bravery-challenged, must take courage to live the powerful, purpose-filled life we were created for.

Thankfully, taking courage is something we can all do, an intentional decision we can all make in spite of the fear we all experience.

Choose Courage

I made this discovery late in my life. I did not learn this growing up in Jackson, Mississippi, which at the time resembled Mayberry, USA. There, my family who loved me, never encouraged me to embark on a path that would require courage. My teachers at school did not encourage risk. I did not hear it preached from the pulpit at the church I attended every Sunday of my life. I personally did not know anyone who was boldly pursuing a destiny that required a vast amount of courage. Everyone I knew was just trying to be good, pay their bills, keep their kids safe, go on a vacation once a year, and retire as early as possible.

Please hear my heart. There is only one thing wrong with that way of life—it is not what we were created for!

The message I received for most of my life, whether covert or overt, was *do not take risks*. As well as *stay safe* and *be good*. Based on how often I heard, "Go to college, get a job, get married, and have kids," I assumed that was my destiny. So at the ripe old age of forty, when I was challenged with the question that would ultimately transform my life:

"Do you have the courage to be you—the you I created?"

My first response was, "Heck no! I don't do scared!" I had been trained to work hard for my comfort zones.

At first, I did not even contemplate the mystery of the question whispered to my soul because of its obvious overtones and implications of fear-producing activities in which I was unwilling to participate. However, ultimately I did wonder why it was going to take courage to be me. Though skeptical and scared, I have to admit I was also intrigued.

For weeks and months, that provocative question seared my soul and tempted me into wanting more. Daily I would hear it whispered. It also created a restlessness inside of me that ruined me for the ordinary existence I had settled for. Though scared to death, an urgency and passion had been planted inside me to discover who I was and what I was supposed to be doing. I longed to know the *me* I was created to be. I wanted to discover if there really was something I was created to do that no one else could do. I longed to change the world.

You can, too.

I pray my words ignite a spark of longing and desperation in you to do just that. I pray this book will propel you into taking the necessary steps required to fulfill your own water-walking, giant-slaying, history-making destiny.

However, I must warn you, destinies of this kind:

- are not safe,

- will make you look crazy,

- require that you often say "I don't know,"

- will cause you to spend time alone, and

- will scare you to death.

It is a journey walked in wild abandon. Steps of faith, not self-reliance, are required.

The Journey to YOU!

If you are serious about being and doing all you were created for, then you must **consult your Creator**— you must consult God. The premise of this entire book is that He designed you. He created you for a destiny too big to imagine or carry out by yourself. That means He alone has all the answers to your questions about you and your purpose. The journey starts with Him—not an abstract, theoretical, cliché version of Him—but one that includes Him as an interactive participant in the process. It has nothing to do with religion but with relationship.

If the concept of talking to God is new to you or feels strange, try starting a journal. Write down your thoughts and questions with regard to your purpose, then record any ideas that occur to you. Talk to your Creator as you would do with anyone you are in relationship with. You do not have to use fancy, formal words. You can be blunt and painfully honest about your doubts, and even be skeptical about the process, if that is how you feel. You do not even have to believe in God for Him to believe in you. What do you have to lose by entertaining the thought that the God of all creation designed you and has a grand purpose for you? It is much better than believing you are of no consequence. I prefer *planned by God* myself.

However, I do admit that hearing His voice and even my own heart is often difficult. It seems easier for me outside in wide-open spaces far from noise, buildings, and people. You may prefer sitting still in a comfortable chair. Listening to music may help you contemplate your existence. There is no right or wrong way to communicate with God. Just talk. **Then** listen for His still, small voice and your own.

The journey to finding the true *you* and what you were created to do is an amazing adventure. Enjoy it!

There are battles to be fought, giants to be slain, and treasures to uncover. It is a journey where logic is challenged, where the ordinary becomes extraordinary, and the impossible becomes possible. It is worth the effort required because, through you and your purpose, lives *will be* changed, history *will be* made and prayers *will be* answered. It is what you were created for.

Is your heart racing? Mine is! Let's get started.

Key Chapter Concepts to Consider:

- You were created on purpose for a very specific purpose.

- You are a water walker, giant slayer and history maker.

- Courage is required and is a choice.

- You being you matters.

- You must consult your Creator for the specific details.

CHAPTER 2

Questions of Purpose

Before I realized I lived in a world where children are sold for sex, my life was extremely comfortable and safe. Some would say I had it all. However, it was not satisfying the longing in my soul to matter and make a difference in this world. As I approached my fortieth birthday, I began asking the not so original questions,

Is this all there is? Why am I here? Do I have a purpose?

It seems just asking them altered the entire trajectory of my life. Suddenly I was longing to be a part of something bigger than I was. I longed for someone to say his or her life was better because I breathe and the world a better place because I live. I wanted to matter. I wanted to make a difference. I just did not know how.

At some point in your life, if you have not already, you will ask the same existential questions that I did. Even though we may be traveling at a different pace, we all end up in the same place, wondering who we are, why we are here, and how to make a difference. This longing is a part of our DNA and is put inside each of us by our Creator to ignite our journey of purpose.

Mine began in the year 2000. The catalyst was my approaching fortieth birthday.

I love birthdays, especially mine, but sometime during the months prior to the celebration, I ran smack into a brick wall. I never dreaded a birthday until that one. My mind screamed and my body confirmed, "My life is half over, and I don't have anything to show for it!"

When I looked back over the first forty years of my life, there was no riveting synopsis. It seemed I had lived the first forty years in pure reaction to a whirlwind of circumstances, whipped around by whatever life or chance threw my way. There was nothing purposeful, intentional, or passionate about my life. Though I was extremely busy, I had not accumulated much in the way of meaningful accomplishments, passionate pursuits, or history-making exploits. This new awareness brought a desperate desire to have all three.

Living on Purpose

After much pre-birthday contemplation, I had an intense longing to matter and live a life of purpose. Even though I looked, I could not find tangible resources offering ways to equip, encourage, and empower me to discover and fulfill my destiny. Although many wonderful organizations exist to feed the poor, heal the sick, and educate children around the world, I could not find many devoting their time and resources to helping ordinary people like me to find their purpose.

Though I had no road map or clue on how to start, with great intention and huge conviction, I vowed to live the next forty years of my life vastly different from the first. Still I had more questions than answers.

What is my purpose? How do I find it? Why am I here?

I asked them to no one in particular. During the night, I lay awake wrestling with these questions in my mind. Neither answers nor clarity came with the morning, just an uneasy feeling, like the one that accompanies a disturbing dream you cannot quite remember. While the nights dragged on, my days seemed to fly by as fast as falling stars. Mirrors confirmed I was aging by the minute. I thought I was having a mid-life crisis or a nervous breakdown. Exhaustion crept in, along with the knowledge that I would never find the answers to the questions of my soul by myself.

Out of sheer desperation and with my birthday fast approaching, I made another intentional decision—I would seek God, not myself or other people, for my answers. After months of restlessness, He suddenly seemed to be the obvious source of enlightenment. I guess that was not so odd since I had believed in Him all my life. I wondered if He really had my answers.

"What am I here for?" "Why am I on this planet?" "Do I have a purpose?" I now asked my questions to my Creator.

I heard no heavenly answers. I saw no burning bushes. The seas did not part. All I got was silence. Maybe I was wrong.

My fortieth birthday came and went. I was frustrated and wondered if my search was in vain.

Ordinary People, World-Changing Feats

During this time of silence and frustration, I made another intentional decision. I began to read the stories in the Bible I remembered from my childhood as part of my decision to seek God for my answers of purpose. I was desperate for answers and thought that maybe this was the way to break the silence and hear God's voice. I assumed I knew all the stories and their endings. I doubted they would be relevant to my quest. I certainly was wrong. They were. I was stunned but inspired by these woefully flawed, often dysfunctional, ordinary human beings God used to impact and change the world. I knew Noah built a boat and brought the animals in two by two so humanity could be saved, but who knew that a couple of chapters later he would fall down, passed out drunk. I knew David slayed a giant with a slingshot and a few pebbles. I knew he later became king, but no one ever told me he had an affair with Bathsheba and then killed her husband to cover it up. Still God called him *a man after his own heart*. I was stunned when I read about a woman caught red-handed having an affair. The law at the time said she should die. Instead, she was offered grace, forgiveness, and a second chance.

As I read their stories, my doubts evaporated. God spoke to me through their stories. I realized He still wants to use ordinary, messed-up people like me to change the world. I wanted that more than anything else in the whole wide world. I wanted to walk on water, slay giants with pebbles, and change history. I wanted the scandalous grace and extravagant love I saw offered over and over again. The small flame of longing was now being stoked into an inferno.

I was encouraged but still restless. My questions without answers felt as if they would explode inside of me. I had to *do* something. I headed to the walking trails near our home and enlisted my dog, Jake, a hyperactive Labrador Retriever, to keep me company. I would literally walk for miles each day, talking aloud, asking my questions and waiting on answers—answers that never came. The solitude was unusual and not very typical for an extrovert like me. I was surprised when I began to enjoy and look forward to it. The wide-open spaces seemed to expand my soul, and I grew more comfortable with the silence offered there.

On those walks, I found it wildly liberating to be free of people's opinions and the need to make everyone in my life happy. My family and friends commented on the change in me. Some even took offense. I had found something so precious that I was unwilling to give it up, no matter the cost. I had found peace. Peace in the stillness. Peace in the whispers. Peace walking and talking to God. After a while, I even found peace with my unanswered questions. Like a magnet, I was drawn out there day after day.

The Courage to Be the YOU I Created

Then on one very ordinary day, on a very ordinary walk, the extraordinary happened and the silence ended. Without any warning or shaking of the earth, I *heard* and even *felt* these words deep inside of me:

Do you have the courage to be you—the you I created?

I immediately stopped walking. Everything around me became still and quiet, even Jake. I looked around. No one was there. Instinctively, I knew the question had not come from me; it came from my Creator. I said the words out loud, very slowly.

Do you have the courage to be you?

My first reaction was, "No!" Then I realized after hours and days and miles on the trail, I finally heard an answer. I knew it had come from God, from my heart. My questions had been answered … with a question. I waited for more whispered words, but none came. The silence returned, but this time it did not frustrate me. I was strangely satisfied and very intrigued with this divine question. I concluded that I must have been asking the wrong question. Instead of asking *what is my purpose?*, I should have been asking, *who am I?* My persistence in seeking was finally paying off.

My walks became longer after *the question*. I was truly perplexed as to why it would take courage to be me. I no longer focused on *what* I was created to do but *who* I was created to be. There was a profound difference between the two. Evidently, the *me* I was created to be was more important than *what* I was created to do. That was fascinating to me.

Clues from Childhood Memories

In the days that ensued and the walks that followed, a divine unveiling occurred. God unveiled me to me. I would ask Him questions about who I was and what I had become. Then I would remember the child I once was. His answers were my memories. I had not thought about the child I was in many years. Now I was prompted to do just that. I could see her; I could even feel her. It seemed she had some of my answers.

I was a well-loved, extremely happy child. I had incredible confidence and was sure of my place in the world. I loved being first at anything and picked for everything. I treasured being the oldest and big sister to my siblings. I took that role very seriously as I did everything else. I cherished my family. I worked hard at being a good girl and never hurting anyone's feelings.

I loved God and told everyone I met that He loved them too. It was easy to believe in a good God when you had good parents. Going to church was my favorite pastime.

I was incredibly intuitive. Helping someone gave me great joy. I was caring and responsible. Though an extrovert, being alone was also comfortable for me.

I did not require much from other people. Someone said I was an old soul. Being with adults and listening to their conversations was much more fun than hanging out with kids my own age.

I loved to tell people what to do and how to do it. I never understood jokes, but I laughed a lot. I loved those who no one else loved. I hated when someone felt left out. At the state fair each year, my dad would win a stuffed animal for me at the basketball throw. After his victory, I was able to choose any prize I wanted. I'd always picked the ugliest, smallest stuffed animal, the one I was certain no one else would choose. I took them home, bestowing upon them a regal name and giving them a prominent place on my bed. I slept with them all so no one would *feel* left out.

At school, I picked friends the same way I picked stuffed animals. I chose the ones never noticed or ever invited home to play. I picked the kids hurt by others with their hands or with their words. I became their protector and cheerleader. In fact, I was a cheerleader!

I was extremely loud, active, and full of energy. I did not know how to whisper or sit still. In kindergarten, I got an "F" on my report card in *naptime* because I talked the entire time. I talked non-stop to anyone who would listen. I even talked to myself. When I talked, I assumed people would value what I had to say and agree with my opinions, even adults. I was always stunned when they asked me to be seen and not heard. I was *shhhhhhhed* very often.

I was a tomboy who loved baby dolls. My athletic abilities were well known in the neighborhood where I grew up. I loved competing with and beating boys in any sport. I threw footballs, hit baseballs, and shot basketballs. I was good at just about any and every sport I tried—gymnastics, diving, softball, even the high jump. I liked to play on a team, and I loved to win. I was always the captain, and I always followed the rules.

I organized everyone and everything. I made decisions quickly and did not worry about outcomes or failures. I wrote poems, kept diaries, and told stories with great animation. I was a leader looking for someone to follow me. I was comfortable on stage and enjoyed having people watch me. I sang in the choir and danced whenever I could. I had no idea that I did not have talent for either. It never once occurred to me to question whether I was liked or accepted; I just assumed I was.

The memories brought a realization that felt like a ton of bricks falling on my head. Somewhere along my life's journey, I stopped being *me*. Sadly, I realized the woman I had become did not resemble the child I once was.

Why? I screamed silently to my Maker. *When did I stop being me?*

A Vow that Robbed Me of My Identity

The answer came within another memory.

I was ten years old. My class had just come in from recess on a hot, humid Mississippi day. We had been playing softball, and as usual, I was the organizer of the game and captain of the team. We had won! When we returned to class, I took my seat on the front row. "Jenny," my teacher whispered, "the principal wants to see you in her office." Instantly, fear and dread washed over me. My palms started to sweat, and I felt sick to my stomach. Only bad kids went to the principal's office and I was a good kid. I inherently knew something was wrong.

As I walked out of the classroom, everyone stared at me, speculating in hushed tones about what I must have done to deserve such a fate. I walked slowly down the hall, my ten-year-old mind wondering the same thing.

I had heard stories from the *bad* kids summoned to the principal's office. Long stays after school, cleaning the blackboards, paddles with holes in them, having to grab your ankles and bend over were all forms of punishment handed out in the principal's office. Yet I was the teacher's pet, and teacher's pets did not go to there.

Walking to the principal's office in shame was *not* a part of that identity. As I inched down the long hallway, I felt my confidence slipping away. That was a new experience for me. My palms were wringing wet, and I kept wiping them on my pants. My mind searched for anything I might have said or done that could warrant this summons.

As I rounded the corner and peeked through the office window, the secretary caught my eye and waved me in. Her smile did nothing to encourage me. I sat in the chair she pointed to, feeling so small. I focused all my attention on my feet swinging back and forth in nervous anticipation.

After what felt like an eternity, I heard my name called rather formally, "Jennifer." No one ever called me Jennifer except on the first day of school, which I quickly corrected by shouting "Jenny!" Now I was scared. I did not correct the principal about my name. I just scooted off the chair and, without looking up, followed her into the room where all the bad kids went. She closed the door.

"Take a seat."

I did, once more staring at the floor. I could not look her in the eye. I felt alone, vulnerable, and unprotected.

She wasted no time with pleasantries and attacked immediately. While I am prone to exaggeration, that is exactly what it was—an attack. *"Aren't you the young lady who wants to be a missionary and go around the world telling everyone that God loves them?"*

Her words felt like an accusation. They were so different from the affirmations I was accustomed to receiving when I announced my career choice. I looked up for the first time. I was confused. She had just announced my dream, the not-so-secret desire of my heart. I passionately gave this answer to anyone who asked me what I wanted to be when I grew up. Something was wrong. At ten, I did not know it was her tone. Her words dripped with sarcasm.

The way she asked the question made the desire of my heart sound like a hideous aspiration for evil. Unfamiliar emotions began to pour into my young psyche: humiliation, shame, and embarrassment. I remember nodding, affirming her question. Though it was the truth, for the first time in my young life I was now embarrassed to admit it. My dream had never been ridiculed, only validated and applauded. This fact caused me to look down and stare at my feet.

She broke the silence with another accusation: "If you love God so much, how could you be so unkind to one of your classmates?" I looked up again. I guess the confused look on my face caused her to continue. She explained how she watched me being mean to Julia at recess during our softball game. Julia was my friend. We had spent many nights together at sleepovers. She did not have any other friends. Everyone laughed and made fun of her because of her weight— everyone except me.

She continued, "You wouldn't let Julia play in the game. You excluded her."

"No!" I wanted to say. "That wasn't true." However, I remained silent while I remembered what had really happened.

The game had already started and the teams chosen when Julia walked up. I would have welcomed her on my team, but she only wanted to bat and did not want to take a turn playing in the outfield. I told her she could not do that because it was against the rules. My dad taught me that. You must take a turn in the outfield if you want a turn at bat. Therefore, Julia decided not to play.

However, I could not say any of this to my principal. I was taught it was disrespectful to talk back to an adult. I was taught to be good. I chose to be silent. That was not like me.

Disturbing Emotions

I wanted to run away from the disturbing emotions unleashed inside of me.

I was in unfamiliar territory. This person in authority called my actions, my dreams, and me into question. She bestowed a new and foreign identity upon me—hypocritical, self-righteous, and unkind. Who was I to argue or question her authority? I was just a child. It must be my fault. I must have done something wrong.

My ten-year-old filter was inadequate and not yet equipped to reject the lies that were pouring into my mind and searing my soul.

It was wrong to be so passionate and vocal about my dreams. It was wrong to talk about God. It was wrong to be a leader. It was wrong to play by the rules. It was wrong to be me.

In those very few minutes behind that closed door, I made a vow that I would never again do anything to make me feel what I felt in that principal's office. I made a vow to stop being me. I did not realize I would keep that vow for almost thirty years.

I told no one about this incident; I was too embarrassed. I just quit. I quit having an opinion. I quit talking about God. I quit leading and started following. I quit writing and telling stories. I quit being on a stage. I did not want anyone to look at me anymore. I began to question who I was. I lost my confidence in being me, because I no longer believed being me was a good thing. I morphed into a chameleon. I became an expert at discovering who and what people wanted or needed me to be. I assimilated and became like everyone else. I did not want to stand out anymore. I stopped trying new things. I stood for nothing. I never said no, which got me in difficult situations, especially with boys, from which I was ill equipped to extract myself as a young girl and teenager. Because I was terrified of those hideous emotions—shame, embarrassment, and humiliation—I stopped being me and became someone else for a very *long* time.

As God pulled back the veil of my past, I saw the woman I had become was a direct result of the silent vow I made many years ago as a ten-year-old child. As I grew older, I grew more fearful of those hated emotions, so I continued to reshape myself. In doing so, I did not know I would lose me—the me I was created to be.

As an adult, I did not believe my opinion was valuable, so I waited for others to offer theirs first. I still talked a lot, but only about things that did not matter and were not controversial. I joined whatever my peers were joining so I would be included and not stand out. I wore what everyone else wore, drank what everyone else drank, and carried on meaningless conversations. I compared myself to everyone and became very judgmental of others and myself. I still went to church, but I never shared my faith. I settled for mediocrity, comfort, and security. I traded in my dreams and desires, assuming this would protect me from ever being humiliated again. It did not. When I stopped being me, I had no idea I traded in my destiny.

Now I finally grasped why I was afraid and could not answer the question, *"Do you have the courage to be you?"*

I did not believe there was more for me. Even more profoundly, I did not believe there was more *to* me.

I finally realized why I was so scared, why I would need courage to be me. Deep in the recesses of my soul where words are not necessary, settling for less was the only thing I knew how to do. I embraced the lifestyle of never believing in or expecting anything extraordinary. I did not know how to believe in me, much less *be me* because I had embraced an identity that was not mine.

Identity Boot Camp

It was as if my Creator now pushed a pause button on my destiny. I was having an identity crisis that needed immediate attention. I was not being me. I had to remove the false, protective identity I had been wearing for years and accept the one that more resembled the bold, confident child I once was. Before I could ever walk on water, I must first learn to be me. I had to make a careful assessment of who I was before I could figure out what I was supposed to do.

This proved to be a long process. I had thirty years to undo. I called this time in my life identity *boot camp*. As I practiced being and believing in me, I heard a new whisper that gave me all the courage I would need.

You were created on purpose for a purpose.

These words seared my soul. Revelation dawned. Me being me mattered. My identity and destiny were related. They were purposefully intertwined. This declaration felt extremely personal and stirred up a longing inside of me that caused all doubts and fear to vanish. Passionately I declared, "Yes! Yes! Yes! I want to be me." I vowed never again to settle for less than I was created for. Then I prayed, "Give me the courage to be me."

It is clear to me now that my fortieth birthday was used to ignite a flame of longing in my heart to be me, nothing more but absolutely refusing to settle for anything less. The drama and subsequent meltdown was not a mere mid-life crisis or random event. It was the divine, invisible, loving hand of my Creator wooing me to my true identity and destiny. Are you being wooed to yours? Do *you* have the courage to be you? It is imperative that you say yes.

As you read my story, I hope it brought to mind the child you once were. It is important to reflect on who you were when you were younger. Consider your personality and your dreams. What did you love to do? Who did you like to spend time with? Consider if you were an extrovert or an introvert, talkative or quiet. Did you like to read, sing, or draw? Did you have a particular talent? Were you competitive? What were you going to be when you grew up? Why?

All these questions can prompt memories that may be important to uncovering your identity and destiny.

Do you now resemble the child you once were? Did you fulfill all your dreams? If so, I am so happy for you! This journey of purpose will go much quicker because you will have less to undo than the rest of us who, for some reason or another, decided that who we were was not such a good idea.

Did you stop being you?

Consult your Creator with these questions and see if He can give you insight into the connection between the child you once were and the adult you have become. Typically, there are clues and connections for your identity and destiny to be found in those memories. You may have made vows much like mine that right now are robbing you of your true identity and world-changing destiny. Take the time to remember.

Key Chapter Concepts to Consider:

- It will take courage to be you.
- You must take intentional steps to discover who you are and

what you are meant to do.

- The child you once were may provide clues.
- You may have stopped being you.
- A false identity may be robbing you of your destiny.

CHAPTER 3

Your Identity Precedes Your Destiny

Your identity precedes your destiny.

You cannot do what you were created to do until you know who you were created to be.

You too probably need an identity boot camp. Have you ever pondered where your identity came from? Did your parents, your friends, a spouse, co-workers, or even your boss bestow an identity upon you? Was it true or false?

From the day you arrived in this world, there has been a never-ending supply of people wanting to tell you who you are—or rather who they want you to be. Our society and the media also want a voice in bestowing our identity. They shout that we need to be rich, powerful, skinny, and gorgeous if we are to be happy. We must be wearing designer clothes and driving a sexy, expensive car to the hottest gathering place in town if we are ever to be noticed and called significant.

This identity sells everything from iPhones to underwear. It is a lie, but we all eventually buy into it.

These types of bogus media advertisements declare we are a society lacking identity. It is a plague on our world. No wonder so many people live lives of quiet desperation and lack of purpose. Who can measure up? Individually and collectively, we have no sense of our unique identity or world-changing destiny. I am especially shocked with people who profess a belief in God yet do not see themselves as valuable, cherished, planned, and loved. Their lack of identity is robbing them of their destiny, and it will rob you of yours too.

Wasted lives. Unfilled purposes. There is nothing sadder and nothing further from God's plans for humanity—and from His plans for you. You must consider *who* you are.

A Child of the Creator

You are a child of God.

If you were raised going to church your entire life, that sentence may not wow you or seem the least bit significant to your identity and destiny. Often mere repetition of a phrase can remove its designed impact and implications. If you have never heard or entertained the thought, it may seem like religious jargon and not carry much weight for you either. However, I promise you this, your entire world-changing destiny hinges on believing and accepting this divine identity.

This is the real secret. The identity secret. This is *who* you are. A beloved child. Adopted into a loving family much larger than your biological one. It is an unmovable, never-changing, irrevocable identity. If we do not realize, internalize, and personalize this identity, then we will never believe we can walk on water, slay giants with stones, or change the course of history for all eternity. We will never step into our destiny.

This identity guarantees that you are loved, planned, and have a place to belong. Your identity does not depend upon the family you were born into or the labels bestowed upon you. Low self-esteem, co-dependent, addict, overweight, orphan, or any other label you struggle under is simply that—a label. It is not *who* you are; it is not your identity. Chosen, cherished, and valued now describe you. That identity guarantees you success in your destiny. Your adoption changes everything! It did for me and it certainly did for my grandmother.

Bessie Richards Smith aka Elizabeth

My grandmother's given name at birth was Bessie Richards Smith. She was born on September 29, 1912, in Hickman, Kentucky to Willford Lee Smith and Maude Ivy Smith. Willford was twenty-two years old when he asked Maude's father for her hand in marriage. Maude was twelve, a common marrying age in the South at that time. The young couple married and moved from their hometown of Memphis, Tennessee to Hickman, Kentucky, so that Willford could find work. Hickman was located on the mighty Mississippi River.

Willford found work on a riverboat, and they settled there to raise their family. When Maude was twenty-one and pregnant with my grandmother, her fifth child, Willford unexpectedly died of pneumonia. Suddenly Maude was alone with four small children to provide for. Her family was far away in Tennessee. I cannot imagine how scared she must have been. There is no detailed account or family stories of this time, but we know Maude gave birth to my grandmother and then traveled back to her family in Memphis. During her journey home, her oldest daughter, Clara, died of scarlet fever.

I do not know how she kept going. Courage? A sense of purpose? Faith in God? I have no idea.

However, I do know when Maude arrived in Memphis, she sought the help of family members. Sadly, no one's financial or living situation was such that they could provide for an additional family. She found no one who would or could take them in. Therefore, Maude did the only thing she could do—she gave her children away.

It was easier finding homes for the boys. Boys could milk cows, chop wood, and pick cotton. So when various cousins offered to take the boys, Maude agreed. What choice did she have? To save them, she had to let them go. The girls proved more difficult to place. My grandmother, the youngest, was placed in an orphanage and put up for adoption.

Maude had no job. Her final task was to find one to support herself. Miraculously, she did, in the same town as the orphanage. I cannot imagine the sense of relief she felt at finding a job, while at the same time, the incredible heartache of giving her children away. My heart longs to know all that she was thinking and feeling as she struggled to survive day by day. Did pain and remorse define her days, or did she thank God for His provision? Did she have faith that God had her and her children in the palm of His hand, or was she angry with Him? Did she believe she had a purpose and a destiny, or was she just defeated? How alone she must have felt. I am sure this was not how she imagined her life. This was not happily ever after.

Meet Eleanor and Benjamin

In another small Tennessee town there lived a loving couple. Though they had everything money could buy, the one and only thing their hearts truly desired—children—was denied to them. While they hoped and prayed for little ones to hold, Benjamin Lee Thomas and Eleanor Glass Thomas lived a generous life, helping those in need in their community. They lived by the motto *"but by the grace of God, there go I"* and responded immediately to any injustices they saw, especially those involving children. Not only did they respond monetarily to the needs they encountered, but they also loved and served the people who had those needs. Though physically barren, they remained pregnant with the possibility of having a child.

Somehow, during the course of their ordinary days, Benjamin and Eleanor heard about Maude and my grandmother. When they did, they left their hometown in Milan, Tennessee and booked a train ride to Memphis to meet Maude. I wonder, did they know it was a journey to their destiny, to their long-awaited daughter, to my grandmother and eventually to me, their great-granddaughter?

They visited Maude and my grandmother three times during the early months of 1914. My grandmother was almost two years old. Benjamin and Eleanor immediately fell in love with her. They invited Maude to visit their home, to see how and where they lived. They continued to make the trip to Memphis to visit her and my grandmother in the orphanage.

After many visits and many hours of sharing their hearts, the Thomases offered to adopt my grandmother. They wanted to give her a new home, a new family, and a new life. They offered Maude dignity by asking her permission, and they offered my grandmother a new name and identity. Was it hard or easy for Maude to say yes? I am sure she was torn. I try to imagine what it was like say good-bye to your child. How my heart aches for her. What unselfish love my great-grandmother Maude demonstrated to her daughter, my grandmother.

The day Benjamin and Eleanor took my grandmother to their home, they adopted her into their hearts. She was their long-awaited daughter. They called her family, giving her their name and a new one of her own, "Elizabeth," which means God's promise. That is who she was to them—a promise fulfilled.

My grandmother loved her new name. She believed it reflected her identity and solidified her destiny. With adoption, her life changed. She was now the beloved daughter of Benjamin and Eleanor Thomas, not an abandoned child left in an orphanage. She had a place where she belonged, and no one could take that away from her. She not only believed she had the same rights and privileges of a biological child, but she saw evidence of it daily, as the Thomases loved her as if she had been born from Eleanor's body. Her identity became one of chosen, redeemed, and loved. Because of that new identity, my grandmother came to believe she could change the world!

You can, too.

I love this story of my grandmother's, my Mimi's, adoption. It mirrors our own. It does not matter how or as whom we started this life. It matters not what circumstances we have been through—pain, death, infertility, poverty, or even abuse. They are no match for the extravagant love and good plans our Creator, our Heavenly Father has for us, His adopted children. We are His and He loves us madly. We cannot change our past, but adoption into God's family can certainly change our future.

Before you can be and do all you were created to, this issue of identity is one that must be settled in your heart and in your mind. You cannot seek your identity from other human beings. Their love for you is flawed and imperfect, and they probably struggle with their own identity issues. Only your Creator can tell you who you are and who He created you to be. Take a long walk and listen for His voice, His confirmation of who you are. Journal your thoughts to the implications of this new identity.

My desire is for you to experience the freedom that comes knowing your true identity as a child of God. Your inheritance is a world-changing destiny that will change you and others. It is birthed out of this identity. This identity is one you can be secure in and courageously act out of, even it takes a while for all the implications to sink in. It certainly did for me.

Facing My Fears

My husband owns his own business; he is a natural gas consultant. We have worked together since the year 2000. At one particular time in our business life, our natural gas supplier informed us that we would have to obtain letters of credit from all of our clients or we would no longer be able to purchase our natural gas. This simple revelation meant we would have no business, thus no jobs or income without those letters of credit. Let's just say this proclamation produced a tad bit of stress in our home.

Prior to our supplier's phone call, I had begun to live out my new identity. I had even made strides in discovering my water-walking destiny. For the first time in thirty years, I was being me and loving it! Until my husband declared that obtaining the letters of credit was *my* new job responsibility. I did not even know what a letter of credit was, much less how to obtain one. My boss (i.e., my husband) offered no advice except *figure it out or we lose the business.* No pressure whatsoever.

The first thing I felt was the old yet familiar fear: *I am about to be embarrassed, humiliated, and ashamed.* It seemed imminent or so I convinced myself. For days, I did nothing. Fear paralyzed me. I felt like I was ten years old again. Suddenly, I had no ability to access my new identity. Until I received an unexpected but much-needed phone call. It was a dear woman and spiritual mentor, Terri Fenwick. She asked, "*What are you doing?*"

Without taking a breath or uttering any pleasantries, I blurted out my predicament. I was blatantly hoping to receive sympathy from her for the incredible burden and responsibility with which my husband had saddled me. She and her husband owned their own business, so I thought she would commiserate with me. Much to my surprise, I got neither from Miss Terri. Instead, she confronted me, *"How many phone calls have you made to the bankers?"*

"None," I whispered in my most pitiful voice.

"Why?"

"I have no idea what to say, what I need, or what I am asking for," I whined. *"I feel like an idiot."*

"What are you wearing?" she asked.

What am I wearing? I could not figure out what that had to do with my situation. *"Uh, my workout clothes from the gym?"*

With a very firm and forceful voice, she said to me something that I have never forgotten, *"Go take a shower right now, then put on your very best clothes and do your make-up and hair. After that, I want you to make ten phone calls to banks this afternoon, expecting with each one that you will receive exactly what you ask for. Jenny, you are the daughter of God, and His favor rests upon you. Act like it."*

Then she hung up.

Terri's words empowered my heart and seemed to add steel to my backbone. She was right. I was a child of God. As that realization once again settled in my mind, I no longer felt like an embarrassed ten-year-old, frightened child. I was no longer afraid of being humiliated. I was nervous, but I was no longer paralyzed. I did what Terri said. I took a shower, and I took courage. Then I made those calls. With each one made, I gained more and more confidence, even though I received many very polite *no's*. However, they did not matter and could not alter my conviction of who I was.

A New Identity

I made a choice. I chose to act out of my new identity. It did not matter what I felt. I could choose. The old fears and negative feelings no longer held me hostage. My true identity was now securely in place. I continued to make those calls with complete confidence, expecting great favor. Finally, through a series of truly miraculous events, we received the letters of credit we needed to continue our business because I had the courage to be me.

Another lesson I learned through that experience is that both my husband and God could see my true identity easier than I could. In the beginning of my journey of purpose, they both believed in me more than I did myself. To prove it, one of them seemed to be throwing me in the *deep end* so I could learn to walk on water.

Identity precedes destiny.

We must stop seeking our identity and sense of self-worth from others, the past, what we do, whom we date, the title before or after our name, or how we perform. None of them matter. We must consult our Creator.

I want to encourage those of you who did not receive the love, blessings, and affirmation from a biological father or mother when you were growing up. I recognize it can be very difficult to have a positive connotation of a Heavenly Father or adopted family if your experience with an earthly one was abusive, distant, or neglectful. It is hard to believe in others, much less yourself, when others have bestowed a false or negative identity on you. If this has been your experience, I am so sorry. How I wish I could change that reality for you.

However, I have good news! While the past cannot be changed, you can change how you think about it and what you believe about it. Old labels and identities can be replaced with new ones that reflect your true self. You are now called beloved. You have a place where you belong. You are planned, unique, and an original. You have a destiny. That is your true identity. Believing it will change everything.

Key Chapter Concepts to Consider:

- Your identity proceeds your destiny.
- You are a child of God.
- You have been adopted into a family.
- This identity will greatly influence your thoughts, feelings, and behaviors.
- This identity is critical in fulfilling your destiny.

CHAPTER 4

Beloved. Belong. Believe.

B eloved. Belong. Believe.
I love these words. They resound deep within me, providing a much-needed melody to my soul. They soothe and encourage me. I want to be called *beloved* by another. I need to have a place to *belong*, where I am a part of something bigger than myself. I long to *believe* that the world, or at least someone, needs me to be me. Beloved. Belong. Believe. These words reveal the secret desires of my heart, all of our hearts.

To live from and make choices out of our true identity, we need to hear these affirming words. None of us are immune to their powerful, transforming work. They are essential ingredients of water-walking, giant-slaying, history-making destinies. When we know we are *loved* and have a place to *belong*, it then becomes much easier to entertain and then *believe* that we have a world-changing destiny. Belief allows the impossible to become possible and the ordinary to become extraordinary. Subsequently, behaviors that do not line up with our true identity—behaviors that are keeping us from our destiny—will suddenly begin to change to align with how we think and feel about ourselves.

Beloved.

In Henri Nouwen's book *Parting Words*, he talks about the identity of beloved.

*I very much believe the core moment of Jesus' public life was the baptism in the Jordan, when Jesus heard the affirmation, "You are my beloved on whom my favor rests." That is the core experience of Jesus. He is reminded in a deep, deep way of **who he is**. The temptations in the desert are temptations to move him away from that spiritual identity. He was tempted to believe he was someone else: You are the one who can turn stone into bread. You are the one who can jump from the temple. You are the one who can make others bow to your power. Jesus said, "No, no, no. I am the Beloved from God." I think his whole life is continually claiming that identity in the midst of everything ... Prayer, then, is listening to that voice—to the One who calls YOU beloved. It is to constantly go back to the truth of who we are and claim it for ourselves. I'm not what I do, I'm not what people say about me. I'm not what I have. Although there is nothing wrong with success, there is nothing wrong with popularity, there is nothing wrong with being powerful, finally my spiritual identity is not rooted in the world, the things the world gives me. My life is rooted in my spiritual identity. Whatever we do, we have to go back regularly to that place of core identity.*

Being called *beloved* is the first process of identity boot camp. Knowing we are loved is essential to believing we matter. Others may or may not have called you beloved. It seems human love is fickle at best and very often is dependent upon our behavior, performance, or ability to meet the needs of another. Loving ourselves becomes our own responsibility. In this effort of discovering our identity and fulfilling our destiny, loving ourselves, even liking ourselves, is paramount to the journey. To love yourself, you must make a careful assessment of who you are and who you are not. It is very interesting how other people will love you to the degree that you love yourself. That is why consulting your Creator is so important to this process. He made you. He delights in you. He can explain you to you—the why of you and what He was thinking when He knitted you together in your mother's womb.

God unveils His intentions for you through the lens of His extravagant love. He sees who you are supposed to be, who He created you to be. He does not see what you lack. He sees your potential and uses His love to transform you into a water-walking, giant-slaying, history-making individual. It will absolutely take courage to be and do all you were created to, but it will also require that you choose to see yourself as God sees you and hear his whisper *beloved.*

You are called beloved; you can choose to embrace the identity. It may be the most courageous decision you ever make. It is very difficult to love someone who does not love himself. It is also extremely difficult to embark on an exciting journey of purpose without loving yourself. Loving yourself may take practice if the concept is new to you. Having a place to belong helps.

Belong.

It seems we human beings have an insatiable desire to belong to something bigger than ourselves. As soon as we are weaned from our mother's breast or the bottle, the desire to attach our independent selves to another person or group begins. Both little girls and boys alike seem to announce their pick of a best friend as soon as they launch into their first social situation. Playdates and birthday parties then ensue.

Today's definition of good parenting demands that a child join as many organized groups as feasible, as early as possible. Girl and Boy Scouts, dance troupes, choirs, martial arts, drama, and every sport imaginable all offer a child a place to belong. As we get older, neither the desire nor the groups diminish. Book clubs, supper clubs, bars, and country clubs are on the menu to meet this need in us as adults. We are so desperate to belong that we are even willing to pay money for the privilege to add our names to a group's exclusive roster. We long to belong, to attach our names to another.

We should not be surprised by our strong need to belong and our aversion to being alone. We started life literally attached to our mother. We were then birthed into a group, a family.

I am Jenny, the oldest daughter of four children, a single entity. However, I *belong* to a family, a family that numbers hundreds of aunts, uncles, cousins, and grandparents. When we are all together, I truly feel a part of something that is bigger than myself. Being a part of a family provides me with a shared name and identity. Though now married, I was born a *Thornton*. That one word meant that we were resilient, independent, confident, loud, athletic, and hard working. We even had a family motto, a collective identity: *We bend, but we do not break.* I can see glimpses of myself in the generations before and after me. It feels good to be connected to this group. When we are together, the longing to belong is appeased, at least for a time. However, being in one place at the same time is very difficult because we are all now scattered across the United States.

The movies we love often highlight this longing to belong. Do you remember the classic line from the movie *Jerry Maguire*? To this day, it is one of my favorites. Tom Cruise's character whispers to Renee Zellweger's character, "*You complete me.*" Every woman who heard those words at the movie theater gasped as her secret desire was broadcast on the screen so simply and clearly from an actor's lips straight to our own hearts.

Romantic love, belonging to another, is something we all believe will complete us. Marriage was designed to give us that sense of belonging. It was to be a place where two separate, unique individuals came together to become one, and from that oneness each entity was to be enhanced, new life formed, and a family created. In my own marriage, I have been so fortunate to experience just that. However, I have also been divorced. I know how difficult it can be when separation occurs. It is a pain-filled process for everyone.

Friendship is another profound way I personally have experienced unity that creates a sense of belonging. Many have said that friends are the family you get to choose. I totally agree.

There are people in my life on whom I have bestowed the identity of *my friend*, but that title woefully lacks the ability to describe what they mean to my heart. One of the kids in our clan coined the phrase *God-family* to describe friends who become family. Time and distance cannot diminish the bond and the oneness we share. These friendships are divine and I believe also created *on purpose for a purpose*. We belong to each other. We regularly share our hearts and holidays, burdens and bread, joys and sorrows. We generously serve, love, and give to each other. We share every aspect of our lives. These relationships help me not to feel like I am all alone in this world. These people encourage me to be and do all I was created to. They believe in me. I belong ... until one of us moves away, gets divorced, or the relationship becomes broken. Then I feel alone again.

When healthy, all of these attachments and relationships *can* provide us with a much needed sense of belonging and an identity intertwined with others. However, they only seem to meet our need to belong on a temporary basis. It does not matter how many groups we belong to or identify with, each of us will find ourselves, at one time or another, alone or lonely, divorced or estranged, left or abandoned. This is incredibly painful and can breed a host of emotions lethal to your newly discovered identity.

That is why God adopted us into his family and provides an irrevocable place for us to belong. This place is not based on efforts or performance. He loved us first. He chooses us and offers a mysterious completeness that other human beings and groups can never provide. I learned this the hard way, and you will probably have to as well. People will never complete me. Your relationships will never complete you. People, and our relationships with them, are imperfect, just as we are.

People alone will never meet our need to belong. When we grasp this truth, it takes the pressure off our relationships and we can just enjoy them. We stop the frantic search to belong.

A bride and groom. Families. Friendships. All these relationships were to be a glimpse, an imperfect copy, of the original design God intended for us to experience in relationship with Him. He wants to give you a permanent place to belong so you are no longer sifting through the rubble of earthly relationships looking to a mere human being to provide only what He can. As I learned this lesson, my relationships with people got stronger because I no longer depended upon them to validate me. I know I have a place where I belong. I know that I am never alone. I know my identity and that I have a world-changing destiny. Do you?

You must look to your Creator to solidify this truth within you. You too are called beloved. You too have a place to belong.

The next step is choosing to believe.

Believe.

Did you know that what you believe could have nothing to do with truth? Your behaviors, choices, and actions could all be based upon a lie or multiple lies that you have internalized as truth.

Psychologists call these erroneous beliefs negative *core narratives.* Established early in our childhood, they result from a negative or traumatic experience that greatly affected and shaped our choices and behaviors. Inevitably, these beliefs become deeply rooted within us, providing a lens for how we view others, our Creator, the world, and ourselves. They become the unconscious programming in our brain from where our behavior originates.

Our positive beliefs and core narratives do not pose many problems for us. However, the negative or false beliefs we obtained from past experiences can distort truth, limit our behaviors, and entice us to settle for so much less than we were created for. Left unexamined, they become our engrained, default behaviors and habits, which rarely align with truth.

The Psychology of Belief

In my work with victims of sex trafficking, I have read numerous books written by professional counselors, therapists, and psychologists who specialize in human behavior and trauma. What I found greatly influenced my own life.

You must change the way you think
before you can change the way you feel,
which ultimately changes how you choose to act.

It all starts in our minds. Your mind is the battlefield over which your emotions, your actions, and reactions are produced. Your thoughts produce your emotions, which produce your choices, behaviors, and actions. It is so very simple. We act upon that which we believe—even if it is not true.

I remember helping my boys with their fourth grade world history homework years ago. We laughed at the *truths* believed by the majority of people during Columbus's day. What they called truth, we called silly—even to fourth grade boys. The people's fears, we quickly determined, were based on unproven truth. We examined their beliefs and, in light of what we knew to be truth today, judged them to be lies.

1. The world was flat, and if you tried to sail to the edge, you would fall off the edge.

2. If you sailed near the equator, your skin would turn black.

3. There was a great sea monster that would eat you alive if you sailed a certain distance from home.

We all laugh at those truths—now. They seem ridiculous—now.

However, long ago, many people believed and based their choices on these commonly held truths, despite the fact they were completely false. Their beliefs produced an emotion, fear, which caused them to make a choice to stay very close to home. Their false beliefs produced self-limiting behaviors that kept them from exploring the world—that kept them from their destiny. That is, until a man came along and courageously and publicly challenged the widely held "truth" of the day. He changed the world. And you can do exactly the same if you begin to examine, evaluate, and challenge your own truths.

Earlier I told you my story of the day I stopped being me. As a ten year old, I had an experience that impacted me in a negative way. When I was subjected to the principal's ridicule of my dreams and values, I felt I had done something terribly wrong and for the first time in my life I felt embarrassed and humiliated. In that moment, I made a silent vow *never* to attempt anything that would cause me to *feel* those emotions again. That negative experience caused me to make an incorrect assumption. *I* was the embarrassment. There was something wrong with *me*. It was always *my* fault. Those emotions were so strong that I agreed with the assessment.

Did you catch that? I agreed. I had an experience that produced a thought or an assumption about the situation. Strong, negative emotions were produced that helped persuade me to come in agreement with that assumption. That agreement produced such a strong belief that whenever I thought about, it produced those very same negative emotions that swayed my choices and behaviors.

All this happened with lightning speed in my brain. My thoughts produced my emotions that ultimately influence my will, my choices, and behaviors.

When I agreed with the assessment, it became a belief that produced the very emotions I was running from. Embarrassment and humiliation. I was embarrassed to be me. Though unconsciously, I began a systematic reprogramming of myself. Those negative emotions influenced and produced self-limiting behaviors for most of my life because the belief was buried in my little girl's heart. It went unexamined for over thirty years. However, my behaviors betrayed the belief I had about myself. Soon I had predictable, default behaviors ready to erupt during any potentially embarrassing situation. The lies, and subsequent behaviors, robbed me of my destiny for years—and if left unexamined, yours will, too.

Default Behaviors

Let's break down the process that I have described. At the center is an experience. That experience produces an assumption telling us whether the experience was good or bad. In our minds, we then come in agreement with that thought. At that moment, the agreement produces a belief that has nothing to do with truth.

From that point on, whenever we think about that experience or belief, an emotion is produced that is in line with our belief.

Therefore, what we think and then how we feel will produce a behavior in line with those beliefs and feelings. This process repeats year after year, faster and faster, until that behavior becomes a default one—a behavior to which you give no thought. It has become a knee-jerk yet predictable action that occurs in predictable situations. You may not even remember why.

Here is a visual to help you connect the dots.

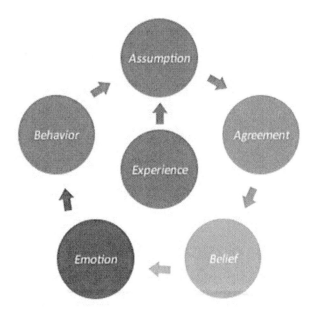

Now let us break the sequence down into smaller components.

We have an experience where assumptions are formed. We then either agree or disagree with that assumption. Based on that decision, a belief is formed. Where and when was truth examined in this scenario? Nowhere. Truth has not been introduced at all.

Now consider the following.

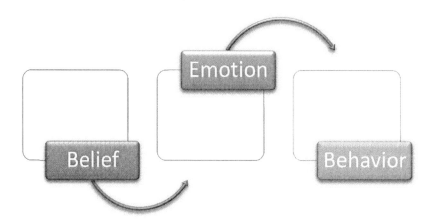

That belief produces an emotion that constructs our behaviors. We do not even have to think about them. Our brains just keep speeding up the process until those behaviors become default, knee-jerk reactions when we sense the emotion.

Think of it this way. A newly purchased computer has an internal software program. It has two operating modes, default and design. The default mode creates actions that automatically happen in certain situations without the operator issuing a specific command. It is easy because it has been programmed.

The design mode is much more complicated. To invoke all the complex applications of the software, for the computer to do all it was created to do, the extensive operating manual or the actual creator of the program must be consulted.

Do you consult the manual when you buy a new computer to optimize performance? Not me. I like quick, easy, and automatic. Unfortunately, for many years, I lived my life that way and my default behaviors kept me from all I was designed to be. Yours may be, too.

We are not much different from a computer. We too have default and design modes. We are extremely complex with great potential, but at the same time have the ability to operate on autopilot doing less than we were designed for. We have the ability to proceed throughout our day acting and reacting to stimuli and situations without much thought. We do this because our default mode is much simpler than our design mode. We have been programmed by our culture, our family, and our experiences. We have become comfortable with our familiar, predictable, and automatic behaviors even if we do not necessarily like them.

We act as if we have no control of them. But that is not true. That is a lie. We can literally take every thought captive before it becomes a freight train wreaking havoc in our lives. Our default mode is what keeps us from our destiny. It is crazy to keep doing the same things over and over again while expecting a different outcome. Yet we do.

Again, the positive reactions and behaviors are not the problem. The negative core beliefs or narratives are what will keep us from being and doing all we were created to. We must get off autopilot. We must examine our programming. We must dig deep. We all have behaviors we want to change, and when we muster up the courage to try to change those behaviors, we fail because we have not challenged the belief that is producing the emotions that helped construct the default behavior. We get frustrated and quit because we do not see the results we long for. We come in agreement with the lie that we are failures. We hate the emotions that belief produces, so we vow to live with our unwanted, self-limiting behaviors. Around and around we go on this merry-go-round of defeat, never being and doing what we were created to.

We as humans focus and spend so much time and money trying to change our behaviors. We try to lose weight, quit smoking, stop drinking, and more, but so many of our behaviors are typical symptoms of deep-rooted emotions that spring from false beliefs or lies implanted in us, typically during our childhood. I found when I began to examine my negative, unwanted behaviors, I could trace them all back to a lie or a label that someone bestowed upon me or a lie I had bestowed upon myself. However, I discovered if I wanted to change a behavior, I first had to identity the feelings and negative beliefs associated with it. Then the behavior became easy to change by replacing the lie with the truth.

We must ask why. We must be authentically self-aware. We must be mindful of the stored experiences and the beliefs they were produced that may not be true. The *why* of the belief is the key to change. It is the bull's-eye we must hit. My behaviors and emotions were easy to identify, but they cloaked the belief. To determine whether my beliefs were true or not, I had to consult my Creator. I made the decision that I was tired of living out of my default mode; I wanted to operate from design. It was a rigorous process that yielded great results in my life—results that can be replicated in yours.

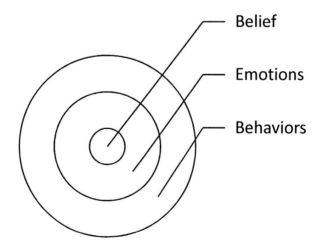

I started with the obvious—my unwanted, default behaviors. I examined my avoidance of anything that had the potential to produce the feelings of embarrassment or humiliation, which can be just about anything except breathing. What are yours? The negative, default behaviors that may be keeping you from being you. Write them down. To identify them, pay close attention to your intense emotional reactions to seemingly benign situations, situations where you react or overreact without cause. Anger, rage, sweaty palms, racing heart, and abject fear are all clues to situations that do not warrant those reactions. Do not gloss over the behavior with rationalizations; instead, begin to ask *why* of your Maker. It is imperative you examine these negative narratives to determine if they are clouding your identity and limiting your destiny.

If you would have asked me ten years ago to go on a stage, make a presentation, or speak to a group of more than four people, all of which I now frequently do, I would have run screaming for the hills. I literally became physically ill at just the thought. That seemed an overreaction. Why? I did not know. I never once questioned it; I just avoided it like the plague, until I had the courage to examine it.

When I began this journey of uncovering my identity and discovering my destiny, I realized I avoided many things that I once loved as a child. Things like athletic competitions, having an opinion, speaking up, and being on stage. Deep in my brain, I believed it would be embarrassing to lose, have a different opinion, or, God forbid, have everyone look at me and freeze with nothing to say. Irrationally, I argued with anyone about anything because I believed it was embarrassing to be wrong. These scenes were all too risky for one as frightened of embarrassment as me, so I avoided them or I went on attack mode. All of these behaviors were default; they required no thought on my part but happened automatically if I sensed potential embarrassment or humiliation. They stemmed from the erroneous belief that I was an embarrassment. I constantly felt unsettled in my soul because any activity or conversation had potential for the feared feelings. My behavior betrayed my belief about myself.

What would happen if you examined your negative beliefs? Can you change them? Can you apply truth and stop them from limiting your behaviors and robbing you of your destiny? Would your life really change? Yes! Yes! Yes!

A core narrative always begins with *I am*—negative or positive. We are going to focus on the negative.

- ☐ I am an embarrassment.
- ☐ I am unplanned.
- ☐ I am of no value.
- ☐ I am unattractive.
- ☐ I am unworthy.
- ☐ I am unintelligent.
- ☐ I am ugly.
- ☐ I am an accident.
- ☐ I am unlovable.
- ☐ I am insignificant.
- ☐ I am the problem.

Do you see how any of these statements could bestow a false identity upon us *if* we come in agreement with them? When we come in agreement with them, they become a belief. These negative and untrue beliefs produce strong emotions and feelings that we begin to act out of. Your behaviors will always betray your beliefs. Let me explain it this way.

If you believe you are unlovable, you will feel unlovable and eventually act unlovable. If you believe you are unintelligent, you feel stupid and will act that way. If you believe you are ugly, you will feel ugly and begin to display ugly behaviors. If you believe you have no value, you will feel insignificant and invisible and begin to make choices that reflect that belief and those feelings. All those behaviors, after a while, become second nature to you. They become your default mode.

Are light bulbs going off? Any flashes of lightning? Is the haze clearing?

Your behaviors stem from who you *believe* you are. What is extremely frightening is the fact that these beliefs may or may not be true. You must examine them.

I did that very thing. I had gotten so tired of overreacting to the insignificant. I hated my reactions in certain situations and could not understand the *why* behind them. I hated being afraid of things that I once loved. I finally became so weary of settling for less than I was created for that I was now willingly to take the time necessary to examine my negative core narratives and expose them to truth. I knew I could not trust myself or another person for the truth, so I consulted my Creator.

Where were the lies? When did they start? What is true about me? I asked the questions and journeyed the process. It was truly life changing. I remembered the false identities and negative labels bestowed upon me by others and by myself. *Too* loud, *too* bossy, *too* embarrassing; the message I received and the lie I believed was clear— I was *too much*. During this process, I began to see the ways I had intentionally begun to dumb myself down and limit my own potential with my negative beliefs.

You are too much, or the other lie, *you not enough*, seem to be two very common negative core narratives bestowed upon people and greatly limit their behavior. Neither is true! We must stop this merry-go-round of negative thoughts, beliefs, feelings, and behaviors if we are going to be and do all we were created to be and do.

First, examine your default, unwanted behaviors, the ones that make no sense but are repetitive. They are usually pretty obvious. Next, identify the emotions associated with that behavior. Do not ignore or run from them. Your feelings are the link between your behavior and the belief which may or may not be true. Our goal here is to expose the lie, not make you feel bad.

Here are some examples to get you thinking:

Unwanted Behavior	Emotion Produced
I *always* **walk out** *when I feel angry*	**Anger** produced the unwanted behavior.
I *always* **quit** *if I feel embarrassed*	The feeling of **embarrassment** caused the quitting.
I *always* **lie** *if I feel worried*	Feeling **worried** pre-empted the lying.
I **steal** *when I feel inadequate or do not measure up to others*	Feeling **inadequate** rationalized the criminal behavior.
I **cheat** *on tests when I feel stupid*	The feeling **stupid** caused the unethical behavior.
I **sleep around** *when I feel undesirable*	Feeling **ugly** produced an unhealthy choice.
I *always* **eat too much** *when I feel sad*	Feeling **sad** caused the overeating.
I *always* **drink excessively** *when I feel stressed financially*	**Stress** produces the excess.

Now see if you can determine the belief that caused the emotion that produced the behavior. Remember, we are focusing on the negative and unwanted ones. Pay attention to statements that begin with *always, no one,* and *never.* Sentences containing those words can provide clues to negative programming. Again, behaviors and emotions are much easier to ascertain than hidden beliefs. At this point in the process, it is imperative you consult your Creator.

Erroneous Belief

I believe I will always hit someone if I get angry, so I walk out during any confrontation or argument.

I believe I will always be laughed at or embarrassed if I try something new, so I quit, or worse, never try.

I believe I will always hurt someone's feelings with the truth, so I become worried and then I lie.

I believe no one will like me for myself; I feel inadequate, so I steal things to make me seem cool.

I believe I will never go to college; I feel dumb, so I cheat on all my tests.

I believe I am not pretty and will never marry, so I feel undesirable and sleep with any man who shows interest in me.

I believe I will never be happy, so when I feel sad, I eat too much to make the feeling go away.

I believe I will never have enough money, so I feel overwhelmed and drink to forget.

These are examples to get you thinking. Can you see how any of these erroneous beliefs can produce negative feelings and subsequent behaviors that could keep someone from being and doing all they were created to? It is much easier to see the connections when we write them down. Please do not worry if you cannot make all the connections right now. Some of my own discoveries and connections took a great deal of time to uncover.

As I promised you in the beginning of our journey together, I am trying to put tangible steps together in order to expedite your time line of uncovering your true identity and fulfilling your destiny. However, your Creator provides the ultimate connections and timing. For now, it is okay to have some gaps and blanks. Trust the One who made you. He will provide all your answers at just the right time.

There is one last step in this process. You need to see if you can remember what incident or experience produced your inaccurate belief or beliefs.

When I was younger, I had multiple negative experiences and disappointments. We all do. However, I discovered there was really only one where I made a vow that caused me to stop being myself. You may also just have one incident or you may have multiple ones. We are each unique, and there is no exact formula that applies to us universally. Consult your Creator for any experience or experiences where you made a vow that has had the greatest impact on your identity and could right now be robbing you of your destiny.

Below are some more examples to get you thinking. I highlighted the incident below that caused the belief, which produced the feelings that prompted the behavior.

Past Experiences

*When I was in the fifth grade I got so angry during dodgeball that **I hit another child with my fist.***

*When I was in junior high, I tried out for the basketball team. The **entire school laughed at me when I shot the ball at the wrong basket.***

*When I was younger, **I told my sister she was a bad dancer, which was true. She cried, said I hurt her feelings,** and she would not play with me anymore.*

*When I was little, **I did not have many friends,** so I watched a lot of television. On the shows I watched, kids who had a lot of cool toys seemed to always have a lot of friends. **I vowed to do the same.***

*When I was in first grade, **I was diagnosed with a learning problem. I had to go to special classes**. I thought I was stupid.*

*My brother told me **I was ugly and that no one would ever want to marry me.** I believed him and started doing anything for boys to notice me.*

*My teacher told me I had a critical personality and that I would never by happy. I told my mom and she baked cookies. **I ate them all and felt better.***

When I was little my dad always yelled about not having enough money. He said it was my mom's fault. She always drank when he said that.

These imaginary incidents, if they happened years ago in imaginary childhoods, would have produced very real, negative core narratives that would have induced vows or assumptions which produced beliefs and feelings that influenced a lifetime of negative behaviors.

> *I am violent, **so** I will never be in a relationship.*

> *I am embarrassing, **so** I will stop being me and be someone else.*

> *I am hurtful, **so** I will only tell people what they want to hear even if it is a lie.*

> *I am alone, **so** I will use things to buy me friends even if I have to steal them.*

> *I am stupid, **so** I will never try hard then I cannot fail.*

> *I am ugly and have no value, **so** I will let others use my body.*

> *I am unhappy, **so** I will eat to numb my pain.*

> *I am inadequate, **so** I will drink to numb the pain.*

The core narratives and lies always start with *I am*. The vow or subsequent assumption that comes afterward always begins with the word *so*. Do you see the connections in my imaginary scenarios?

When you read these examples, you may be thinking how ridiculous and simplistic they sound, just like the ones from Columbus's day. Other people's fears and lies often do. However, our own seem very real and greatly influence our lives. I am certain there is something your Creator wants to reveal to you about you that will jumpstart your journey of purpose. This may be it! Be open to the process. Ask the questions. Start with examining any of your behaviors or habits that you would like to change and see if you can determine the incident that produced a false belief and negative emotion. Determine if you made a vow that you believed would protect you but instead hindered you from being you.

The Truth Changes Everything.

Your beliefs may have nothing to do with truth but *can* change what you believe—with truth.

Your Creator has all of your answers. He knows your design mode because He created it. Just as with our computer analogy, you are much more complex, created for so much more than your default, destiny-limiting behaviors. He knows who He created you to be.

When I asked God, "*Who am I and who did you create me to be?*" My thoughts traveled down an entirely different path than my familiar, negative core narratives. Instead of *I am an embarrassment and I am too loud,* I heard *you are vivacious.* Instead of *I talk too much,* I heard *you are a good communicator. I am bossy* was replaced with *you are a strong leader. It is all my fault* became *you are victorious.* On and on it went until I had a new vocabulary. Every negative thought and subsequent lie I believed about me was exposed, examined, and then replaced with truth by the One who made me. These were words I wanted to believe about me and for me. These words were the ones I now came in agreement with. It took much discipline. I wrote them down on five-by-seven cards and read them out loud every single day, three times a day for months before they silenced the lies I had believed for years.

- I am a good communicator.
- I am a strong leader.
- I am not an embarrassment.
- I am victorious.
- I am vivacious. (I love that word!)
- I am a child of God, created on purpose for a purpose.
- I have a destiny.
- I am beloved.
- I belong.
- I am planned.

This was my new identity. My job now was simply to believe. In the beginning, believing was a daily choice, not a feeling. As I practiced my new truth aloud, my thoughts began to change and miraculously so did my feelings! When that happened, the self-limiting, unwanted behaviors began to align with the truth I chose to believe about me. When the written down words became my truth, I began to confidently act and operate out of my design mode. It felt unnatural at first. It even took a great deal of courage for me to leave the known for the unknown. However, when I did, I discovered many activities that once scared me to death were actually the very ones God designed as a part of my identity and destiny. Though I took baby steps at first, even the people in my life began to notice the changes in me as I began to make strides toward my destiny. I even started speaking on a stage and loved it.

Beloved. Belong. Believe.

This is truth. You are a *beloved* child, created to impact and change this world. The truth is that you *belong* to something bigger than yourself. This truth gives you the courage and capacity to examine your negatives narratives and get rid of self-limiting behaviors so you can choose to *believe you* were created to change the world.

You are a water walker, giant slayer, and history maker. It is your destiny. Believe!

I highly recommend you get a package of five-by-seven cards to write down your new truths. Your default mode is very familiar and easy, but it is not your design. Consult your Creator for your truth, combine it with faith, and watch those unwanted behaviors change.

What about you? What will you choose to believe? The answer to that is so important and life altering because you *will* become what you believe. Therefore, this journey requires faith in what you do not see. Just a few thoughts about faith before we end this chapter—it is important.

Many people use the words *faith* and *belief* interchangeably. Dictionary.com defines it as:

Belief that is not based on proof.

Sounds rather unintelligent, doesn't it? The Bible has a definition I like much better:

Faith is being sure of what we hope for and certain of what we cannot see. Hebrews 11:1

That is what we have been talking about in this chapter. Having confidence in what we *cannot* see at this moment but what we believe will be. That is having faith in yourself. That is what your identity boot camp is for, to convince you that you are who God says you are and that you have what it takes to do what He has created you to do.

Get your truth cards out and daily repeat the words you have written. Negative or positive repetition has the same outcome; it will become a well-worn path in our brain that will produce emotions that will affect our behaviors. It can be a negative rut we are stuck in or a positive path to our purpose. You can reverse the process of negativity with truth. With this truth …

Before time began, you were created on purpose for a purpose. You have a great destiny awaiting you.

Examine what you believe and then why you believe it. Change your truth. You do have the courage to be you!

Repeat these words with me until you have the faith to believe:

I am beloved. I do belong. I have a destiny. I will believe.

I want to give you an invitation and then the permission to be you, the you God created. Sow this truth into your heart:

I am unique, an original work of art. I am fearfully and wonderfully made.

Before time began I was known, planned, and loved. I am no accident. I am meant to be. I have a purpose and a destiny.

Now that is the truth.

Key Chapter Concepts to Consider:

- Being called beloved is the first stage of identity boot camp.
- People will never meet our need to belong.
- What we believe could have absolutely nothing to do with truth.
- Negative or wrong beliefs can produce self-limiting behaviors that can rob us of our destiny.
- We can change what we believe if we ask why we believe it.

CHAPTER 5

You Were Planned

When I was twelve years old, I uncovered a family secret—about myself.

One weekend when I was at my grandmother's house, I was thumbing through the family Bible with my cousin Tracy. It contained all the recorded births, deaths, and marriages of all our family members for generations and generations. It was fun reading all the names and looking at the dates. Toward the very end, the date of my birth was listed, as was the date of my parents' marriage. However, the year of my parents' marriage was wrong—or so I thought.

I immediately showed the error to my grandmother. She was the logical choice since she was the matriarch of our family and the only one allowed in this generation to record data. She reviewed the data and then promptly guaranteed me that the date of my parents' marriage was correct. No argument. This was recorded truth written in her own handwriting.

I told my cousin that something was very wrong. The math could not be correct. I counted the months again. May, June, July, August, September, October, and then November. Seven months—not nine—between my parents' wedding date and my birth. The realization slowly began to sink deep within me.

My parents had to get married. My parents had to get married because of me.

I was unplanned.

I did not tell my parents I had learned their secret. Being the child I was, I did not want to embarrass them, especially my mom. I instinctively knew that talking to her about this new truth would do just that.

The news did not rock my twelve-year-old world because I was an extremely well-loved child. I had felt wanted my entire life. The discovery of my parents' secret did not alter or undermine that truth. It was secure in my heart and a positive core narrative of mine. My parents may not have planned my birth, but throughout my life, they loved me extravagantly. Therefore, at the ripe old age of twelve, I buried the secret. (Well, I may have let it leak to my siblings.)

However, just a few years ago while I was going through my own identity boot camp searching for my identity and destiny, I was talking to my seventy-five-year-old aunt, Dean, my mom's oldest sister, on the phone. I knew she had been at the hospital the day I was born. She was another who had loved me madly since she first learned of my existence, planned or not. I shared with her the secret I had kept most of my life. Without hesitation, she proclaimed truth that traveled two thousand miles through the phone line, straight to my heart. "Oh, darlin', you were no accident. Your life is proof that you were planned by God—on purpose for a purpose."

Warm waves of love flowed over me, on me, and through me. I caught my breath. They entered into the core of who I was. I knew she was right, but I was surprised just how badly I needed to hear them. I did not wrestle with this truth or have the need to examine it further. I just received it, agreed with it, and believed it. Despite the details of my conception, I knew deep within me that my life was planned on purpose for a purpose just as my aunt said.

Yours was, too.

Planned on Purpose

Has anyone ever said these words to you? *You were planned. You are not an accident.*

They are words it seems we all need to hear. I know I did. This positive core narrative is one we all need to embrace and believe.

It does not matter what the circumstances were surrounding your birth; that does not change the fact that you were intentionally planned with a specific purpose in mind designed just for you. Since the beginning of time, you have been tenderly thought of and intimately loved by your Creator. That is no accident.

What is your first response when you hear these words? Is it easy for you to believe them? If, like me, you had loving parents, then yes, it is probably easy for you to accept and embrace this truth about yourself. However, if your parents abandoned or abused you, or never showed you tangible proof of their love, then these words may cause a terrible ache in your heart. If that is the case for you, I am so sorry. It is not my intent to cause you any pain. This one area of identity boot camp may take incredible courage on your part. You may need a large dose of courage to believe a loving Creator planned you. I believe there is evidence of that fact.

If this is a struggle for you, re-read the last chapter to determine if there was an experience from early in your life that caused you to believe a lie that became a negative core narrative. It may be one that has taken root in your heart causing you to feel bad about yourself, thus producing default, self-limiting behaviors that will keep you from accepting a positive identity and water-walking destiny. If so, it will be very difficult for you to be and do all you were created to if you cannot accept and believe the truth that you were planned. Consult your Creator. Ask Him to lead you to the evidence of His love. He says that even though your mother and father have forsaken you, He has not and He will not. Before time began, you were planned. You are necessary to this world. You are as unique as a work of art. You have been designed to be and do something that no one else on this planet can be or do. Look for the evidence. Look to the actual day of your birth. Are there clues there? Mine had some.

I woke up early on the morning of November 7, 2003. It was my forty-third birthday *and* my eleventh wedding anniversary. (Yes, I got married on my birthday.) The day began much like any other: a cup of coffee and a prayer for guidance, provision, and protection. The normal rhythm of an ordinary day—or so I thought. A friend of mine called me to say happy birthday, but she added mysteriously, "God has a special surprise for you today." That was intriguing. No one had ever said anything like that to me before. I was in the third year of my purpose journey, finally realizing my true identity. Daily I was filled with child-like expectancy. Maybe my destiny was just around the corner. However, today was my birthday.

The reason I woke up early that morning was to savor the sweet silence of my sleeping children and to open my birthday cards and presents alone. It was a luxury to sip my coffee and read the words lavished on me from my family members and friends without little boys running around. I had almost an hour to myself before I heard the stirring of my precious boys. One last card. Hurriedly, I tore it open, hoping I could read it before the boys made it downstairs screaming, "I'm hungry!" The words on the card went straight to my spirit.

"On your birthday, I wish for you one perfect moment when you are utterly yourself,

when you are convinced you are God's own child … when you realize that everything is within your grasp."

– Maya Angelou

I felt Maya had written those words just for me! They filled me with expectancy. How I wanted to ponder them for hours, but I did not have the time. The boys were now dragging their daddy half-awake down the stairs, intent on bestowing homemade cards, birthday wishes, and many kisses on me.

As I cooked breakfast for my boys and my husband, yes, moms cook on their birthday, my mind was visualizing and planning the day: lunch with my girlfriends, phone calls from far away family, grocery store, takeout for the kids, and then a romantic evening of dancing with my husband. I was looking forward to a date with my husband because it was also our wedding anniversary. I love to dance.

With the kids off to school and a slew of my errands completed, I had a few minutes to shower and get dressed before meeting my friends for lunch. I grabbed the mail before running out the door, just in case more birthday cards arrived. (I love words, especially words to me about me.)

Among the pile of bills and catalogs, I recognized the handwriting on an envelope buried at the bottom of the pile. It was from one of my most favorite people in the world, my Aunt Dean, the one who was there on the day I arrived into this world and reminded me that I was no accident. She had never once missed sending me a card on my birthday. Her cards were always accompanied with a long newsy letter about our family. I assumed today was the same. I anxiously opened her card. Strange. Instead of the long letter I had grown accustomed to, I pulled out a short note in her handwriting.

"I remember the day you were born like it was yesterday. It was such a special day. November 7th. You and Granny share the same birthday.

What? Granny and I were born on the same day? How was this news kept from me for forty-three years? The woman who was not related to me by blood, the woman who had rescued my Mimi from the orphanage and called her daughter, who adopted her into her family, was also born on November 7. I had no idea. Instantly my heart recognized the significance of this news. Time felt like it stopped. It was *evidence* that I was planned. Even the day of my birth was no accident and had great significance. What an amazing birthday gift! I felt like I had just won the lottery. My soul was saturated with love. I burst into tears with this new knowledge. I felt unique, special, and significant. Though I was going to be late for my own birthday lunch, I was determined to savor this moment.

Seldom had I felt this way … except maybe on my wedding day.

I glanced down and touched the thin gold wedding band I wear on my ring finger. It was Granny's wedding ring. My Mimi had given me the ring when I was a teenager. She told me it had belonged to Eleanor, her adoptive mom. She told me how much Granny had loved me, and that she was at the hospital on the day I was born. (I guess she neglected to tell me we shared the same birthday.)

When I first put the ring on my finger, I marveled that it fit me perfectly. I treasured having this tangible remembrance of the woman who rescued my Mimi from an orphanage. It had stayed hidden carefully in a jewelry box until my handsome husband placed it on my finger on our wedding day, November 7, the day Eleanor and I were born. As I touched our ring, I marveled that she was there on the day I was born, welcoming me, her great-granddaughter by adoption, an unplanned child, into the world on the day of her own birth. It all felt so significant.

At that moment, I believed—no, I *knew*—that before time began our birthdays and destinies were designed to be intertwined. I knew it was a sign from my Creator, evidence my life was planned. I wondered what this woman whispered to me, what prayers she prayed over me at my birth. Did she pass something sacred from her heart to mine in those first moments of my life? I gaze at an old black and white photo of her and I that sits on my desk. She is holding me in her lap. I am a year old. Mimi is standing with us. I am laughing. Three generations created by choice, by adoption, not by blood, and all planned before time began.

I savor even now how incredibly special I feel, just because of the day of my birth. Chosen. Planned. Loved. Set apart. Unique. Destined for something special, something that only I can do. It seems it all began generations before I was even born. My Creator must have known I would need this additional dose of identity bestowed upon me before I was launched into my destiny. My friend was correct. I had been given an extraordinary gift on my birthday—the knowledge and proof that not only was I planned but even the day of my birth was significant. It felt like a kiss from heaven.

On Purpose for a Purpose

This new truth resonated within me. I agreed and believed. My feelings were changing as I gained confidence in my new identity. These beliefs and feelings were changing my behaviors.

As I began to believe that I was born at this time, in this place, for a very specific reason, I saw how my parents, grandparents, and great-grandparents were responsible for giving me a firm foundation to stand on. I saw how the ceiling of their life was my floor. I realized the rich heritage I had received from the generations before me—

generations of strong, water-walking, giant-slaying men and women who with faith believed their Creator for their truth, who took courage to be and do all they were created to. Their past had something to do with my future. I could not wait to find more evidence. I was being wooed into my destiny.

I hope my story encourages you. God has surprises planned for you too. Surprises that will to confirm your uniqueness and bestow your identity in such a personal way that leaves you feeling special, known, and loved. Your heart is being prepared to receive the details of your destiny. Like Maya Angelou, I, too, wish for you one perfect moment when you are utterly yourself, when you are convinced you are a child of God and everything is within your grasp.

Expect tangible, surprising evidence along your journey to help convince you. Look for proof until you find it. Some clues to your identity and destiny are revealed as surprises just when you need them, but others you must go looking for. Have you considered your name for clues? Do you know its meaning? Names often offer important clues to our identity and destiny.

We human beings have been bestowing names and using them to give significance to lives since the beginning of recorded history. In distant eras, names bestowed upon children often reflected their parents' feelings or the circumstances during or around the time of their birth. Those feelings or circumstances could be good and bad. At first glance, some of the names people are saddled with at birth could be a burden or just plain unkind. We need to dig to find our answers.

If you have ever had children, you know the weighty responsibility that comes with bestowing a name upon another human being, a name they will carry throughout their lives. It is a source of great conversations, and even controversy, during the nine months of pregnancy. Almost immediately, the masses of family members begin asking, "What are you going to name the baby?" Everyone has an opinion, but no one gets a vote except the parents. Names, just like identities, are bestowed upon us and can provide clues to "who we are."

We Southerners are especially fond of family names. We use our father's names as first names, we create double names from our grandfather's names, and frequently use our mother's or even grandmother's maiden names in the mix. Just ask my sons.

Some of us are named from books our parents loved or from the movies they watched. My dad named me Jenny after a movie he saw and loved while my mom was pregnant with me, called *The Portrait of Jenny*. While I have never seen the movie, I always loved hearing how I got my name. It was a part of my unique story. My Aunt Dean thought Jenny sounded more like a nickname and bestowed the name Jennifer upon me and my birth certificate. No one has ever called me Jennifer. That name never fit me. It sounded too girly and formal for me since I was a tomboy.

When I first discovered the meaning of Jennifer, it confirmed my suspicions that I was not one. Jennifer means *fair one* or *white beauty*. I was neither fair, as in *fair maiden*, nor have I ever felt particularly beautiful. I was a Jenny. However, I hated the definitions I found. Either Jenny was a *donkey* or *a washing machine*, a spinning Jenny. My middle name is Lee, inserted by my Mom. It was the middle name of my great-grandfather Benjamin. It gave my mom and me the same initials. J.L.T. Jenny Lee. Yikes. I have never loved my name; I thought it was ordinary and plain like me. It is interesting how my name and my self-concept became one in the same. I longed to be called Victoria or Alexandra. Those names sounded so daring and exciting to me. Things I believed I was not. Until my journey of purpose.

I never contemplated how much weight a name carries, from an identity and destiny perspective, until a trip I took back to my home in the San Francisco Bay area after moving to Sacramento, California. I was going to be with the women who had served as my righteous girlfriends—women on a similar journey of purpose. I was their leader. We had met together once a week for seven years. I missed them. Unbeknownst to me on that day, the new leader of the group had been researching the names of each group member—mine included. When I arrived, these precious women surrounded me with love and bestowed a gift upon me I will never forget.

Jenny, your name means courageous, grace-filled, and straightforward. God wants you to know He sees you, that He has called you by name. Your name is the essence of your life's message.

The words were like living water and liquid peace poured over my soul. I was stunned. Even my name was not random. I found this new truth to be intoxicating, life changing, and transforming, especially on this day during a particularly difficult time in my life. It was one where I was fighting to keep my identity intact and my dreams alive.

Sobbing ensued as these words went straight to my heart. Courageous. Me? I had been scared for most of my life. Paralyzed by the fear of embarrassment. However, somewhere inside of me I remembered the active, courageous little girl I once was. In an instant, the past and present collided in my mind, giving me confirmation of who I was created to be. Hearing that description of my name on that day was like a voice cheering me on, telling me not to quit, because I was created to be courageous! Even my name was not without purpose.

Later, when I was alone, I pondered the other words, *grace-filled* and *straightforward*. I wondered what they meant. Like the word *courageous*, *graceful* or *grace-filled* was a not description many would use to describe me. I tend to be more like a bull in a china shop. *Straightforward* was rather perplexing also. I had always been scared of hurting someone's feelings. Because of that fear, I would never come right out and say anything direct. Then I had a revelation. A whisper from my Maker. *I created you to be a communicator, a courageous leader, whose words would be straightforward but filled with grace.* My heart almost burst. That is who I wanted to be. My soul recognized the truth and instantly I chose to believe.

I was so excited over the revelation produced in my name that suddenly I wanted to *be* courageous, grace-filled, and direct. I loved this new identity! Remember our lesson from the previous chapter? What you *believe* produces *feelings* that result in how you *behave*. The formula was working for me. When I believed these new words about me, they produced feelings of confidence that were about to erupt into new positive behaviors in my life. I could not wait to be me, but I also wanted everyone I knew to experience the same thing. Because of that, I became curious about the names of the people in my life, who I loved. Revelation continued as I researched my family and friends' names. I was shocked at how the definitions of their names represented many facets of their personalities.

What Is in a Name?

I found my father's name incredibly appropriate: Charles, a mighty warrior. He is a mighty warrior, but I had married one as well. My husband is Charles Michael. Michael is a fierce, warrior angel per the Bible. Both men have a strong, fighting spirit that will not allow them to ever quit, turn tail, or run. They have both infused, inspired, and encouraged me to be me by their love, their courage, and tenacious spirits.

I was amused, but not surprised, that all my sons, Steven Austin, Michael Dean, and Benjamin Kemp also have champion, victorious, or warrior descriptions to one of their names. They are each strong young men who do not give up easily. When I studied their other name, it was unique to them alone and very appropriate. One is a peace-filled green valley, another is called beloved, and the other is royal or regal. I was fascinated by how accurately their names described aspects of their personalities. I was fascinated because I did not research the meaning of their names prior to naming them

My middle name, Lee, is translated as "a green valley or a place of rest," which is my favorite color and my favorite place in the world. It is also the same meaning as the names of my beloved great-grandfather, grandfather, aunt, and middle son—*Dean.* Being in each of their presences is like walking beside still waters near a green valley. Janey, my mom and niece's name, means "God is gracious." It is true. My mom is one of the most gracious human beings on this planet. Her middle name is Lucy, meaning "bringer of light." Everyone in my family would agree that my mom is a gracious light bearer in each of our lives. Again, I was wowed by the meanings of our names and the part they played in our identity.

Now it is your turn. Have you ever searched the meaning of your name? Are you intrigued? Many books and websites give the origin and definition of names. However, be diligent; dig for the root meaning of your entire name. Some of us receive immediate revelation about our names and identities; however, I have met others where the correlation was not so obvious. Do not be discouraged if this is the case when you search for the meaning of your name. Consult your Creator to determine if your name can give you clues to your unique identity and world-changing destiny.

When your name is called, hear the hidden whisper of your Maker.

You are known. You are loved. You belong. You were planned.

This should fill you with wonder. I challenge you to believe and agree.

I pray you are beginning to understand the depth of your Creator's love for you. I pray you are beginning to catch a glimpse of how carefully you were imagined, planned, and uniquely created on purpose for a purpose. I pray you are starting to feel your Creator's delight as you embark on this journey of purpose.

Key Chapter Concepts to Consider:

- You and your life were planned.
- You are necessary.
- You are tenderly thought about and loved.
- You may need courage just to believe.
- Your heart is being prepared to receive the details of your destiny.

CHAPTER 6

Body Work

You are a unique and complex creature. You are extraordinary. You have a body, a soul, and a spirit. There are parts of you that are seen and parts that are not. There are parts that are healthy and some that may be unhealthy. Understanding all parts of *you* is essential work for being and doing all you were created to do. Making a careful exploration of yourself *is* identity boot camp and must become a priority in your life. It is an exercise in loving yourself, and it is imperative for successful water walkers, giant slayers, and history makers.

Your Body

Let us start with making a careful assessment of our bodies—the tangible, outward part of who we are. The part of us that is recognizable. It is the part everyone can see and touch. It includes but is not limited to our eye color, the color and texture of our hair, our height, our shape, and our weight. It includes our organs, muscles, cells, and bones. Each body is an amazing, unique, and fascinating creation. However, not all of us love our bodies, and because of that, not all of us take care of our bodies.

You may need a great deal of courage to read this chapter. Do not quit now. I encourage you to continue. This may be the most important truth you receive. What you believe about your body may or may not be true. However, your feelings are produced by that belief. If it is negative, they could be causing you unhealthy habits or behaviors. We are not going to start with discussing those. We are going to start by determining if the core narrative you have about your body is based on truth or a lie. If we are to be and do all we were create to, then we must be honest about our bodies. We need truth. However, we need truth that does not come from the TV, a magazine, or our culture. Those views are grossly distorted.

I recognize this is a sensitive subject. You have the courage to face truth; I know you do. You are a water walker, giant slayer and history maker in the making. You can do it.

We were formed in our mother's womb. It was an optimal place for growth. Everything we needed to survive and thrive was there. After we were born, others cared for our bodies then, and as we grew older, we were taught to do the same. Eventually it became our responsibility to take care of ourselves, to be good stewards of this incredible gift we have been given—our bodies. When we were young, it was much easier.

If you grew up going to church, you could not have missed the sermons on being good stewards of our lives and our money. I did not. However, I do not remember lessons from the pulpit on being a good steward of my body. There were sermons on the danger of smoking, alcohol, and drugs, but they had nothing to do with my being healthy. I was told not to have sex before marriage, but I do not remember anyone preaching on exercising more and eating less if I was to be and do all I was created to.

As I became older, my body image was dictated by movie stars and models. I believed that to be beautiful, I must be thin. Thus began my life long rollercoaster ride of trying to look like people on television or the movie screen. My health was never once a consideration. It was all about the size of my jeans until I began to contemplate my identity and destiny.

Eventually during this journey or purpose, I was faced with the question, "How in the world am I ever going to carry out my purpose in this life if I am tired, lethargic, and overweight?" My answer came quickly and simply—I will not. I cannot.

Friends, please hear my heart on this. I am not talking about the issues with regard to our bodies that we have no control over, such as genetics. I am talking about the things we do have control over—diet, exercise, and sleep—and the choices we make in those areas. On my journey, I had to take ownership of those choices. Again, I found it much easier to change my unhealthy behaviors if I examined my beliefs and any experiences that caused them. I am five feet five inches if I stand up very tall. I have what "they" call a muscular build. I am never going to be a willowy supermodel. Did I also mention I am in my fifties? That may also be a deterrent to a modeling career.

Friends, we have to see our bodies as vehicles to our destiny. We cannot and will not be able to do all we were created to until our bodies are healthy and operating at optimal performance for our age. We need to consult our doctors as well as our Creator. We need to get take courage and be honest. It is common to talk about and even condemn those who use excessive amounts of alcohol or take drugs. However, we seem to avoid talking honestly about the abuse of eating too much and exercising too little. Doctors are very concerned, telling us repeatedly that we are an overweight society and that ignoring the fact is going to kill us. Please, again hear my heart. I am not addressing this issue to make anybody feel bad or hurt anyone's feelings. I am addressing this issue because I believe your body and your health can keep you from embracing your true identity and fulfilling your destiny. This subject must be addressed directly. There is too much at stake, but I promise to do it gently and gracefully. Remember, I am your biggest fan!

I do not want to shift from being your identity and destiny coach and encourager to being your weight loss coach. However, if unaddressed, this issue will give you a false identity and has the power to rob you of your destiny. I believe this struggle of weight affects more of us than does excessive alcohol or drug abuse. We know the health risks associated with that. However, we need to educate ourselves on the health risks associated with being overweight. This issue is not to be avoided. At the very least, you are not living life as you were created to, and at worst, you are shortening your life span considerably.

Consider this quote:

> *If you are overweight, you are more likely to develop health problems, such as heart disease, stroke, diabetes, certain types of cancer, gout (joint pain caused by excess uric acid), and gallbladder disease. Being overweight can also cause problems such as sleep apnea (interrupted breathing during sleep) and osteoarthritis (wearing away of the joints). The more overweight you are, the more likely you are to have health problems. Weight loss can help improve the harmful effects of being overweight. However, many overweight people have difficulty reaching their healthy body weight. Studies show that you can improve your health by losing as little as 10 to 20 pounds. (See "Do You Know the Health Risks of Being Overweight?" www.healthgoods.com.)*

This is great news. Yes, being overweight can cause health problems, but you can immediately improve the harmful effects by losing weight. That is truth. Agree with it. Believe it.

Confession

I have to confess that at the writing of this book, I am *moderately overweight* according to my doctor, heading to *slightly obese* if I do nothing. These words can quickly become more labels and core narratives that cause negative emotions which will become self-limiting behaviors if I accept them and do nothing. I have to treat them as a diagnosis and not a label. Then I am immediately encouraged that only a slight loss in weight can improve my physical health and reduce my chance of disease. Stepping on a scale makes me feel bad and produces negative actions. Signing up for boot camp—fitness boot camp—makes me feel strong and encourages me to make choices that improve my health.

My weight has roller-coastered for years, but there was only a ten- to fifteen-pound variance—until I reached my fifties and that number became an alarming thirty to forty pounds. When the number is low, my self-esteem is high. When the number is high, my self-esteem is low. I have wrestled with this since I quit smoking in 1994. I decided twenty years ago to stop slowing killing myself in that particular way. It was a good decision, but I received a new problem. Now that I did not smoke, food tasted so much better. Therefore, I ate more. I am not an emotional eater. My problem is that I am a Southerner and we just like our food fried and with lots of butter.

In my home I am the cook, so I cook what I like. I cannot understand why you would spend any time cooking something that does not taste good. Therefore, each night I am confronted with a plate full of food that I love, prepared just the way I like it. Sadly, each night my family of men get up from the table and I am left there buttering just one more piece of cornbread. When I dare to look at what a "normal" portion is, I am shocked at the small portion of food "they" expect me to live on.

I hate this struggle. I hate feeling so defeated in this area of my life. I needed new beliefs and agreements if I was going to live out my destiny.

Here is a truth I had to admit and then believe. In this area of my life, I could not do it alone. I needed discipline and accountability. Weighing myself alone only produced negative feelings and bad behaviors. I needed someone to hold me accountable for my choices. You may too. It does not matter if it is Jenny Craig, a fitness boot camp, a personal trainer, Weight Watchers, or one of the numerous other weight loss programs out there. If you do not have the money for those, then enlist a friend to exercise with and weigh in together regarding your results. Yes, that means letting another person see and record the number on the scale. I am not terribly fond of this disclosure, but I love the results. It works.

My old mistaken core belief raises its ugly head every time I contemplate accountability in this area of my life. I feel that icky embarrassed feeling in the pit of my stomach every time I must publically weigh in. However, now I confront the old erroneous belief and lie: *I am an embarrassment.* "No, I am not!" I now scream. I am unhealthy at this weight, that is true, but I have the power to make choices to change it. Quickly that truth produces feelings of wellness that surround me. I can succeed. I quickly realized the truth that no one else really cares how much I weigh. They are much more concerned about their own weight. Disclosing my weight to others takes courage, but when I do, my accountability partners encourage me and cheer for me. They celebrate my successes, challenge my choices, and give me a swift kick in the butt when I need it. They believe in me when I do not believe in myself. I want to be healthy. I want to feel strong. To do that, I embrace and include others in this part of my journey. I do not want anything to keep me from discovering my true identity and fulfilling my destiny. That is my motivation!

Living Your Destiny

As I type these words, my dad is in Africa, feeding widows and orphans. He is seventy-seven years old and has been to Africa more than eight times within the last eight years. He has built a church by hand, planted so many gardens I have lost count, dug water wells (again by hand), walked miles in the bush, and hiked up mountains just to fulfill what he believes is his purpose. To do this, he must take a twenty-six-hour flight from Jackson, Mississippi to the continent of Africa. Once he gets there, he prefers to sleep on a dirt floor in an African hut deep in the bush. He rides for hours in the back of a gravel truck to get to his destination instead of renting a car. He squats over a hole in the ground for a toilet, and he eats food that has not been approved by the FDA. He even hiked Mt. Kilimanjaro several years ago! At seventy-three, he was the third oldest person in the world to make it to the top of Kili. Nineteen thousand feet. My dad is walking on water and smack dab in the middle of his destiny.

My dad can do all of this because he has taken care of his body every day of his life. At seventy-seven, he cannot rely on a good gene pool. He has practiced, and continues to practice, good stewardship of his body. Those widows and orphans in Africa need him to be and do all he was created to so they can eat. What if he could not go? What if he was not physically able to do what he has been called to do? The answer is quite simple: People would starve to death.

This mind-boggling statement can apply to all of us. If we are not being and doing what we were created to be and do, then there is an unmet need and an unanswered prayer in this world.

My friends, not only your Creator eagerly awaiting you to be you, so are other people. My dad's ability to make these trips to Africa is a direct result of how he cares for the body he has been given. He exercises, watches what he eats, gets plenty of rest, and does not put unhealthy things in his body. It is not complicated. It just is not that easy for me.

I could spend the rest of the chapters in this book coaching on just physical health. We could set goals to achieve a healthy weight and healthy lifestyle. We could set up accountability and motivation exercises. We could and we should, but there are numerous weight-loss and exercise programs aimed at addressing our body. I urge you to pick one. Do whatever you need to do to get healthy. Make a goal. Get help. Make a careful assessment, find out what you need to be doing, then *just do it!* Determine a start date. Again, I would suggest that you consult with a doctor if you have not exercised or had a check-up in a while. Medical websites abound and can provide you with accurate information on beginning a journey to good health.

Some of you may not have a weight problem, but you have not had a physical in years. Call your doctor. Get your blood work done. Check your blood pressure. Make sure you are as healthy as you can be. If you are in pain, go to the doctor. If you need to have surgery, schedule it.

Last January my knees were killing me. I went to the doctor, and he took x-rays and told me arthritis had eaten away all the cartilage in my knees and that I would never run or jump again. I was devastated. I was too young for knee replacements, and I decided I was also too young to stop running and jumping. I found a new doctor who did a procedure that allowed me to get back to the gym sooner rather than later. I continued losing weight, but I am more excited that I am still running and jumping. Second opinions are a beautiful thing. Never mistake your doctor as your Creator.

Ladies, some of you may be suffering with the symptoms of

menopause. I had a terrible time. Scattered thoughts, weight gain, hot flashes, no sleep, and exhaustion were a few of my symptoms. My poor husband. I was fortunate; he was supportive and encouraging during this very difficult time for me. I had so many different people offering me different versions of truth. I refused to believe I had to spend the rest of my life feeling bad. I confided in friends my age. I saw three different doctors. I tried many different options until I found one that worked for me. You can too. Call your friends, call your doctor, take supplements or hormones. Do not believe the lie that your life is over. You still have choices. I did for a year and it changed my life. I went from tired, hot, weak, irritated, and overweight, to fit, strong, active, and excited to go to fitness boot camp. Your life is not over. Fight for your health. If I can do it, so can you. Be a good steward of your body. You need it on this journey of purpose.

What is your goal? When will you start? Call your doctor now and set an appointment. Now for the scary part. Call a friend, someone who loves you and believes in you. Tell them of your commitment. Ask them to hold you accountable in a very practical way. Have them call you and ask you if you exercised each day. Keep a food journal and read it to them daily. Text them your beginning weight and measurements. Update them weekly. Find other ways to be accountable to your partner. You *can* have victory in this area of your life. Believe it and you will begin to feel it. (By the way, saying *I will start tomorrow* or *I will start on Monday* is not a commitment and is not a choice that will produce results.)

My prayer for you today is that you will have the faith to believe you can have victory in this area of your life. I long for you, and for me, to choose to believe we are fearfully and wonderfully made as we take responsibility for the care and stewardship of our bodies. I want you to have all the strength and energy required to be and do all you created you to be and do.

Key Chapter Concepts to Consider:

- Your body is your responsibility.

- To be and do all you were created to, you must be healthy.
- Being overweight is not embarrassing; it is just unhealthy.
- Accountability is often necessary to see change in this area.
- Your body can keep you from your destiny.

CHAPTER 7

Soul Talk

You consist of three different but distinctive parts. Together they make up the whole of you. To be and do all you were created to, these three parts—your body, soul, and spirit—need time, attention, and care in order to be healthy. It can get rather confusing when we talk about our souls and spirits, the unseen parts of us. Some people use the word *soul* and *spirit* interchangeably. However, after my own personal research seeking to make a careful assessment of who I am, I have come to separate the two words—soul and spirit. Here is what I found.

My soul is me. My soul includes my heart, my mind, my emotions, my will, and my beliefs. My soul can be swayed, influenced, and inspired. It is my personality, my likes, and my dislikes. I can love and hate from my soul. My soul is all the parts of me you cannot see but greatly influence me. My soul was created just as my body was.

The Parts that Make You YOU

I am an extrovert who also loves my *alone* time. I love to talk. I am loud. I love Mexican food. The Blues make me dance. I love to dance. I hate games. I love deep conversations—soul conversations. I love the sun. I hate the cold, but I love to see snow. I choose still, quiet streams over the roar of the ocean. I love trees. I love green. I love to be up high, looking out into wide-open spaces, but I hate heights. I love to hike. I hate extreme sports. I hate to go fast. I like to feel safe. I like to feel strong. I love to start and complete tasks, but I hate managing them. I hate structure. I like to stay at home. I love vacations. I would rather decorate my home than my body. I love being with people. I love having people in my home. I love solitude. I love change. I hate to be bored. I have child-like faith. I am generous. I hate being wrong. I am embarrassed easily.

That is me, a glimpse inside my soul all in a couple of paragraph.

What about you? Have you ever given much thought to your soul? The *who am I* question? What you like, what you do not like? Have you ever made a careful assessment of who you are? If you have not, do so now. Ask people who know and love you to describe you in a paragraph much like I described myself in the one above. This is always a fun and interesting exercise for people. This exercise is not to be an encouragement to run to others for your identity but a way to prove how very often your self-perception can be clouded by the negative narrative, which, for most of us, began in our childhoods. I am hyper vigilant in examining my default behaviors. It is an area of intrigue in my own self-assessment. The emotionally healthy people in our lives can often help us spot a negative core narrative that is buried deep in our soul. They are able to hold up a mirror in which we can truly see ourselves.

I have never really struggled with low self-esteem or lack of confidence (except with that whole weight thing), but I am always surprised when someone compliments me or describes me in a positive or flattering manner. For some reason, I feel bad instead of good. I *feel* I need to immediately list all my flaws. With their compliment, I feel like my disclosures would allow them to see that I do not deserve a compliment. I *believe* I do not deserve a compliment. Notice how my feelings were associated with what I believed and they had nothing to do with truth.

One of my friends pointed out this habit of mine. When I examined my feelings instead of ignoring them, they were the bridge that led me back to a belief that had become a core narrative. I discovered my brain, unbeknownst to me, was rewinding the tape of my lie back to when I was ten years old walking down the hall to the principal's office. Though a default reaction with no conscious or intentional thought on my part, I still felt the emotions associated with the belief that I have done something wrong, which produces the assumption that I do not deserve compliments. I do not even realize that my brain is looking for every failure, fault, and bad decision I have ever made as evidence. Embarrassment is the feeling that produces the conclusion that I am not special but flawed. I am aware of none of this except that I instantly *feel* bad and those feelings produce the default behavior or deflecting habit I had acquired. These feelings had the power to wreak havoc in my life and continue limiting my behavior. This belief that I always do something wrong will rob me of my destiny. I will never attempt the water-walking, giant-slaying feats I was created for if I allow this belief to remain.

We give more weight to our feelings than we should. We must stop trusting our feelings as truth. Feelings are subjective. They come from thoughts that can be negative or positive, truths or lies. They come from circumstances, experiences, and interaction with others, many of whom do not know their own identity and destiny. Feelings can change in an instant, depending upon many variables.

Do you really want to base your identity on something that is ever-changing?

My feelings sometimes resemble a roller coaster, screaming up or careening straight down with a few hairpin turns. At my age, menopause alone can cause a monumental change in emotions from day to day and sometimes hour to hour. I certainly do not *feel* like I have a great destiny on many days. When those feelings creep in, I get out my truth cards or go for a long walk with my Maker. I have learned my feelings are not reliable indicators of truth. We must stop basing our identity on ever-changing feelings and start basing them on a never-changing God. I made this life-changing choice and it transformed my identity and launched me into my destiny.

Who We Are—Not What We Feel

Dear mighty warriors and righteous girlfriends, we should never base our beliefs, our truth, and certainly not our choices or actions on our feelings! Yes, we are emotional beings; we all *feel*. However, to base your value, your self-worth, and your choices on your feelings is a recipe for disaster, and, as I stated previously, may have nothing to do with truth.

In the last twenty-four hours, I have probably felt countless emotions: some pleasant and some not so pleasant, some based on the reality of a situation, and some based on my inaccurate belief, assumption, or perception. Thus, feelings cannot be trusted to make decisions unless first examined to ensure the belief on what they are based on is true! Our feelings are not good indicators of reality.

As I have said before, feelings have nothing to do with truth but with our perception, whether accurate or inaccurate, of a situation. They should not be trusted, nor should they be the basis and/or justification for our decisions, our actions, and our behaviors. So many times, I have heard people use their *feelings* as an excuse to not move forward into their destinies. Feelings are deceitful. That might be a news flash for some of you.

But wait a minute. If our emotions and thoughts are not to be trusted, if our heart is not to be relied on, then what do we base our choices and actions on? Simple. Truth. What is really happening in a given situation. What is really going on inside of you that is causing you to act or react. We need to be truthful—gut honest—with ourselves if we want to begin to rule over our emotions instead of allowing them to rule over us.

If we are ever to live out our destinies, we must stop giving so much weight to our feelings. Quite honestly, it does not matter if you "feel" like you are a water-walking, giant-slaying, history-making person; you need to begin to *act* like it. Repeatedly, as I study this topic of emotions and feelings, I am convinced and have seen overwhelming evidence that we have power to make choices in spite of how we feel.

We can choose.

We do not have to be victimized by our emotions, our feelings, or our circumstances. Nothing changes until we change how we think about something. Sadly for some people, long after circumstances change and abuse stops, they are still held captive by their thoughts, which produce negative emotions, which lead to poor choices.

You have a new identity! You are to be a water-walking, giant-slaying, history-making person. That is why it matters how you act and how you respond.

I have taught my children that they have my name and our Creator's name on their backs when they go to someone's house or out in this world—their behavior is a reflection on both of us. Weighty, huh? We must stop acting out of our emotions and resolve to *be* and *do* in spite of how we feel or the circumstances in which we find ourselves. Destinies are at stake. *Your* destiny is at stake.

However, I must warn you, the pursuit of your destiny will cause people to say, "You hurt my feelings," and become disappointed in your choices because you did not put their feelings first. Some people may even get downright mad at you. It is very important that you are aware and comfortable with that. While you cannot control other people, you certainly can control of yourself!

I hope you are falling in love with yourself or at the very least starting to like the way you were made. I pray that you are truly realizing what an amazing creation you are. When you begin to see yourself the way your Creator sees you, the way He created you, then and only then will you believe the plans He has for you.

I am thankful for my friend who pointed out what she thought was just an annoying habit of mine; in reality it was a habit that was keeping me from being me. Sometimes others can see what we cannot. Enlist those you love in your assessment of yourself. They may see negative behaviors you are familiar and comfortable with that required a dose of truth.

Another way to make a careful assessment of who we are, another mirror we can use, is through personality assessments. They offer tangible, objective proof of who you are and what unique strengths, gifts, and talents you possess. They can help you glimpse into your soul. They also can give you a new vocabulary and new truths about yourself.

Assessing Who You Are

> *Hide not your talents.*
> *They for use were made.*
> *What's a sundial in the shade?*
> – Benjamin Franklin

I have listed three of my favorite soul and personality assessments. I highly recommend them to assist you in making a careful assessment of *who you are*. Two of the recommendations require you buy the books to take the assessment. One assessment provides you a code for an online test and the other has the assessment in the back of the book. The third assessment I recommend is online and is free.

* StrengthsFinder 2.0

This is one of my very favorite assessment tools. It focuses on your natural strengths instead of your weaknesses; it highlights what you have instead of what you lack. Since I tend to focus on my weaknesses, this assessment was pure delight. Author Tom Rath shows you how to develop these raw strengths into excellence, but you must buy the book to get the code to take the computerized assessment.

"Do you have the opportunity to do what you do best every day? For years I did not and most people I coach or interview say the same thing. All too often, our natural talents, our strengths go untapped. From the cradle to the cubicle, we devote more time to fixing our shortcomings than to developing our strengths."

StrengthsFinder 2.0 by Tom Rath

According to this assessment, I am a wooer, relater, communicator, activator, and maximizer. What a zany soul combination. I had no idea what those words meant. However, they sounded much better than the descriptions I was accustomed to. I eagerly read the details from the report I received. Truth. The words I read *were* about me. I loved the descriptions of my strengths. Some things I knew about myself, but I would not have called them strengths. I *do* love to *influence* complete strangers by wooing them into deep, meaningful conversations that turn into *relationships* and purpose-filled endeavors. I love *communicating* my passions with my voice or a pen, making quick decisions to advance a plan, while *maximizing* individual efforts that will literally and collectively change the world! I took this words as truth. I began to believe them, feel them and act upon them.

What are you waiting for? Order the book now. As soon as it arrives, I encourage you to take the assessment and let the descriptive words become truth for you. You do not even have to read the book.

* The Five Love Languages

How do you like to be loved? When do you feel loved? This book helped me answer those questions and identify what I needed to embark on this journey of purpose. Live a life of love. It sounds so simple. When we have been loved well, we can love others well. However, many people have not been loved well by the other humans in their life. That is why our Creator has adopted us into His family— to lavish His love on us so we can lavish it on others. I have discovered that on my own I just do not know how to love others well. How do I love them in a way that speaks to the core of their being?

The answer to this question can be found in Gary Chapman's book *The Five Love Languages.* Knowing your love language and the love language of everyone in your life is the most amazing tool I have found in "loving well." Generally, we tend to love others in the way we long to be loved. In his book, Gary not only assesses your own love language but teaches how to love others in their language. I highly, highly recommend this book. Every married couple, every parent, and every friend should read this book. It literally can save relationships. It also helps you love you.

Mr. Chapman's book explained much about my soul to me, things I did not know about myself. I am a *words of affirmation* girl. Long, deep meaningful conversations are my favorite things in the entire world. I do not need flowers or jewelry—just write me a love letter. I do not need someone to sit and hold my hand or go to the grocery store with me— just send me a text or a tweet and tell me I matter. Words are very powerful to me—both words of praise and words of criticism.

One has the power to build me up and the other to tear me down. Now I understand words are so powerful to my soul.

In reading this book, I discovered that my husband and my best friend are *quality time* people. Now everything made sense in our relationship. They could care less if I wrote them a three-page letter or spent an hour talking on the phone to them; in order to feel loved by me, they need to spend time with me. This was a revelation that strengthened our relationships. I am now intentional about scheduling time to be with them so I can love them well. They also love me by writing me a note or indulging my need for long late-night conversations. This assessment was instrumental in helping me have the courage to be me. I believe it will do the same for you.

* The Enneagram

Another of my favorite soul assessments is the Enneagram. It is a tool that has been particularly valuable to me in understanding myself and my default reactions. The free assessment found online at www.enneagram.com. Here is an excerpt from the website:

> *From one point of view, the Enneagram can be seen as a set of nine distinct personality types, with each number on the Enneagram denoting one type. It is common to find a little of yourself in all nine of the types, although one of them should stand out as being closest to yourself. This is your basic personality type. Everyone emerges from childhood with one of the nine types dominating their personality, with inborn temperament and other prenatal factors being the main determinants of our type. This is one area where most all of the major Enneagram authors agree—we are born with a dominant type. Subsequently, this inborn orientation largely determines the ways in which we learn to adapt to our early childhood environment. It also seems to lead to certain unconscious orientations toward our parental figures, but why this is so, we still do not know. In any case, by the time children are four or five years old, their consciousness has developed sufficiently to have a separate sense of self. Although their identity is still very fluid, at this age children begin to establish themselves and find ways of fitting into the world on their own.*

I am fascinated by the Enneagram because it talks so much about identity. I remember the first time I took the test and discovered I am a "one"! I was shocked. Driven by anger? Me? I never get angry. A perfectionist? I am the least perfect person I know. I had to consult my Creator immediately. When I did, He began to show me once again how He carefully created me on purpose for my purpose. I do not get angry when things go wrong or I if do not get my way. I do not feel angry with people very often. I do not get my feelings hurt easily, and I am not prone to spending hours and days to make sure something is perfect. However, I do get angry when situations of injustice, prejudice, and captivity exist in the world I live in—when they are not perfect. I get angry and extremely frustrated when people settle for less than they were created for. My anger creates a sense of urgency inside of me to change those types of imperfections and injustices.

I cannot sit still and do nothing. It is how I am created.

However, at the same time, I am exceptionally easygoing. I love peace and harmony much more than confrontation. I am happy. I have the Enneagram "wings" of peace, harmony, and compassion. It softens the urgency and anger I feel over injustices. The Enneagram was a tool for me to see the contradictions of my soul and my personality as well as the danger of not being aligned to the purposes and plans I was created for. I believe it can do the same for you.

We Are Amazing Creations

We are truly complex beings. When hurting or diseased, our body shows symptoms that require our attention. If we do not respond to those symptoms, our pain gets worse. So does our soul. Like our bodies, our soul needs examination and attention if it is to be healthy. Our soul is more than just our personalities that we assessed; it is also our will, our emotions, and our feelings. When all of these aspects of our soul are healthy, then we can trust our opinions, our assumptions, and our feelings to be road maps to our destinies. If they are unhealthy, then they are suspect and not to be trusted for truth. This one issue—your feelings—can hold you captive in a cell of self-doubt from which you will never escape. I want to dig a bit deeper into our soul. I want to talk about our feelings and how they are impacted by our choices, sometimes called our will or free will. I also want to talk about our needs, our wants, and what we value. All of these are aspects of our soul.

The Impact of Feelings

"I don't feel like it!" a teenager shouts at his parent. "You hurt my feelings," a woman accuses her husband. "I feel worthless," a man confesses after losing his job. "I feel useless," an elderly woman prays. I feel, I feel, I feel. As I type those words I smile, imagining a three-year-old in the midst of a temper tantrum, kicking and screaming as intense emotions erupt and feelings overflow uncontrollably. Dictionary.com defines *emotions* as simply "strong feelings." Interesting. In our culture, we give great weight to our *feelings*—too much, it seems. If we are not careful, our feelings can also keep us from being and doing all that we were created to be and do.

When I speak on this topic, I start out asking the audience this question: "How many of you have had your feelings hurt today?" Consistently, over half the audience raises their hands. You guessed it—the female half.

Yes, we women are guilty of slinging these words around for offenses both real and imagined. The slight that elicits these words can range from "You forgot my birthday!" to "You didn't like my spaghetti sauce." "You hurt my feelings." is definitely a chick phrase and one I must confess I used early in my marriage to manipulate my husband. Yes, I said *to manipulate*. To be honest, I somehow felt empowered when I could cause my husband to grovel on occasion for what I deemed his lack of sensitivity.

What I did not realize at the time was that I was choosing to be offended. That bears repeating. I was choosing to be offended, although I did not realize it. Ninety-nine percent of the time, my husband was not trying to be hurtful; he was just being a man. I did not stop to assess why I was feeling the way I was because I was fixated and determined to make him be responsible for my feelings. Verbal whipping, pouting for days, all the while I was hoping he would figure out why I was so hurt and mad. He never did. Which made me feel more hurt. After a while I figured out this course of action was never going to solve anything. Sometimes it went on for so long that I could not remember what I got my feelings hurt about in the first place. I think that during the first few days of my pout, my husband was just thankful that I was not talking so much, though honestly he had no idea why I was mad at him or that my feelings were even hurt. Around and around we went. At the end of three or four days of silence and one-syllable answers, I finally had to announce to him his great sin and the reason I was so hurt, because he had no clue. If I remembered. It all sounds ridiculous. It is much more than that. It is deadly. It is emotional blackmail, and it is wrong. It kills intimacy. It kills unity. It kills relationships and even marriages. It incites division, causes separation, and will keep you from your water-walking destiny. Your emotions are controlling you instead of the still, small voice of your Creator, the voice of truth.

Emotional Control

We must stop allowing our emotions to control us if we are ever going to live out and fulfill our destinies. It is a lie to say, "I can't help it. It is just how I feel." You may believe that, but it was far from the truth. I was stunned when I began to realize that many individuals are not leading lives of purpose and passion because they are allowing their emotions to be in control. We must take our emotions captive. We must confront them if we are going to be free to be and do all we were created to.

I realize some of these emotions and the circumstances that produce these feelings are strong and scary. We prefer ignoring, numbing, or pretending they are not there over examining them. We actually have the power in our souls to choose to do just that. It is called denial. However, this strategy is a ticking time bomb that will lead to an explosion. Explosions are not good. People get hurt.

Let me say this first before we continue. I know many women, men, and teenagers who are dealing with real oppression, depression, and hideous circumstances. Their emotions are real, overwhelming, and debilitating. If this is you, I encourage you to contact a professionally trained counselor or therapist to help you confront and deal with your emotions and determine your beliefs and experiences that may be causing them. Get help for your pain. There can be very real chemical imbalances in our brain that can intensify existing emotions or even produce feelings we alone cannot associate with an experience or belief. My encouragement is to get help and get healthy. This is loving yourself and dealing with your emotions in a healthy manner. Take your five-by-seven cards of positive beliefs and affirmations with you.

Care for your soul. Confront your emotions. Challenge your beliefs. Courageously take your feelings to your Creator and let Him bathe them in love. Let Him reveal your incorrect beliefs and assumptions— about yourself or the situation you find yourself in. He promises to be bigger than both. As your Creator examines your soul, He will begin to show you your future. You will discover that your dreams and destiny are much larger than your present circumstances and any feelings associated with them. God will reveal you to you. When you choose to believe, your feelings will begin to change and miraculously so will your circumstances. Resolve daily to think on these things. If you do not, your dreams will die within you.

This is *your* responsibility, not that of the people in your life.

While it can be incredibly healing to share your feelings with someone you trust, be careful not hit them over the head or make them responsible for them. They are yours alone. No human being or circumstance can *make* you feel anything. Your brain is doing that. Your belief and your assumptions are doing that.

I have a theory. Most of us fall into one of two camps with this issue of emotions and feelings. Either we are *feeling-givers* or we are *feeling-takers*. I am a feeling-taker. You do not even have to ask me to take your feelings; I will come looking for them.

For most of my life, I have assumed responsibility for other people's feelings. My false belief was produced by my emotions. I hate seeing the people I love in pain. I hate someone being mad at me. I believe it was my fault. We feeling-takers are also called *people-pleasers*. I believed, incorrectly, that it was my responsibility to fix people, assume their emotions, and be responsible for their happiness. Most people who are like me are called co-dependent. Ouch.

Much like false identities bestowed upon us by others, taking on other people's feelings is exhausting. It is like taking a suitcase full of rocks from everyone you meet all day long. It gets heavy. However, the alternative in my mind was that the people I loved were left feeling bad, sad or mad—at me. This made me feel bad. So I tried my best to make them happy. However, it never lasted because people do not stay happy for very long when they do not assume responsibility for their own actions. They are always looking for someone to blame or cast off their emotions. I found people liked it when I assumed responsibility for their feelings. During my own soul assessment, my Creator helped me realize that it takes an incredible amount of energy and focus for me to control my own emotions. Therefore, it is impossible for me to be responsible for my own emotions *and* others'. He showed me that if I continued down this path, I would never be who He created me to be and fulfill my destiny. Sadly, neither would those that I loved. My greatest desire was to daily have the courage to be me, nothing more, but absolutely refuse to settle for anything less, while encouraging everyone who crossed my path to do the same. My behaviors were limiting that possibility. I vowed to change. I accepted this truth and it set me free.

I came to realize that if I am living from my true identity, taking steps toward my water-walking, giant-slaying, history-making destiny, then there will be times when people's feelings will be hurt and they will be disappointed by my actions or inactions. Some people may even get mad at me when I stop putting their feelings above my purpose. I hate that, I really do. It was a hard behavior for me to change. However, the longing to be and do all I was created to became stronger. I have to admit it was also so freeing to know I am only responsible for making choices that lead me to my own identity and destiny. At the same time, I can point others to God for their answers instead of feeling like I am the one who has to produce them. This was a novel concept at the time.

I do not need to have all the answers, and I do not have to make everyone happy and neither do you. ***This is not our purpose.*** It is unhealthy for our souls. If you tend to be a feeling-taker like me, you may have to repeat this new truth several times a day before you can believe it, feel it, and act out of it. Write it on your five-by-seven cards.

Not relating? Then you may be a feeling-giver. You love us feeling-takers. You may not even realize that you look for people to give your feelings to. While it is good and healthy to share your feelings with someone, it is wrong to make them feel responsible for your emotions and happiness. It is wrong to blame another person or even a circumstance for your feelings. This is manipulation. Ouch.

Each of us *must* take responsibility for our own emotions and feelings. We must resolve to *not* be controlled by them—or worse, to blame others. Feelings do not come from people. Our feelings come from our beliefs. Therefore, we can control them by examining the belief producing them. That is how we change them.

You can choose to not be offended. You can choose to forgive. You can choose to examine your emotions and take them to your Creator.

Needs, Wants, and Values

Your soul has unique needs, wants, and values. Identifying them is an exercise in making a careful assessment of yourself. It is another step in your identity boot camp.

There is no one else like you. You are an exceptional work of art. You are special, unique, and original. If all that is true, then why in the world do we strive so very hard for most of our lives trying to look and act like everyone else? We spend more time attempting to reinvent ourselves rather than getting to know ourselves. That is just plain wrong. It is critical that you know you, love you, and value you so that you can be and do all you were created for!

Have you ever considered what you need to get out of bed every day? What do you need to motivate you to be and do all you were created for? What do you need in place in order for you to do your best, to never quit, and to never give up? What do you need to fight for your true identity and destiny?

What about your wants? What do you want out of life? What do you want to be your legacy? What do you want to be when you grow up? What do you want people to say about you after you leave this planet?

Have you ever considered what you value? What is most important to you in life? What is non-negotiable and why?

Needs, wants, and values. Knowing these three things about yourself will accelerate your journey to your destiny!

Needs

Needs are conditions, things, and feelings that you *must* have to be satisfied in life, to be content, to experience fulfillment, and to experience what some would call finding happiness. Often, needs are the things that must be met before you can really get on with life. When we have unmet needs, we tend to get stuck in a rut of a particular behavior or thought pattern and are more susceptible to being sad, depressed, angry, or resentful.

When I say the word *need*, I'm not talking about air to breathe, food to stay alive, and shelter from the elements. Of course we need those to stay alive. I'm talking about the things you *need* in order to be you, in order for you to soar. The needs I am talking about are not selfish ones; they were part of how you were crafted before time began. These types of needs are unique to us as individuals. For some of us it can be acceptance, accomplishments, acknowledgments, compliments, being loved, being needed, being right, having security, clarity, accuracy, comfort, communication, control, responsibility, freedom, peace, order, power, recognition, safety, work, or significance. These are the things that are critical to our motivation, and they are things most of us never contemplate. Think of it as a shot of adrenaline in our arm.

When these needs are withheld, or we believe they are, we can easily fall prey to despair, disillusionment, depression, disappointment, and discouragement—the Big D's! Left unexamined, our unmet needs can stop us from ever being and doing all we were created for. Consult your Creator about your needs. Find out what essential needs you have in order for you to be you.

When I began this process, I believed with all my heart that I needed comfort and security. However, during this process of discovering my identity and fulfilling my destiny I actually found out those needs were false and being placed on me by culture and society. I came in agreement with that belief. I incorrectly believed they would keep me safe. However, when I pursued and focused on them, they actually kept me from my destiny. It was so fascinating to discover through the process of consulting my Creator that even my real needs were put within me to help motivate me and propel me to my true identity and destiny. Ascertaining my needs was a critical exercise that ultimately launched me into my destiny!

Here are a few things I discovered about myself. While you are reading these, consider what you believe you need to be you and then consult your Creator to see if they are true.

I need to matter. I need to know that what I am doing has a purpose and matters in the grand scheme of things. I need to be a part of something bigger than myself. I need to bring people together for a purpose. I need to hear my Creator's voice. I need to lead. I need to speak up. I need courage to be and do all I am created to do. I need to encourage everyone I meet. I need to be doing something. I need wide-open spaces. I need to be in authentic relationships.

I discovered I needed these things like I need the air I breathe. I needed them to be me. What about you? What do you need to be you? Take the time now to journal some thoughts.

Wants

Wants are distinct from needs. We are often made to believe that needs are necessary and wants are selfish. I disagree. Wants are conditions, things, or experiences that you feel would optimize your life. Wants can come from past experiences, upbringing, or advertising. Wants, just like needs, can be the motivator that gets you out of bed every day. The things you want, when processed with your Creator, can give you a glimpse into the destiny you have been created for.

Define your wants and then review periodically.

At one point in my life, I thought I wanted to be a fashion model ... let's just say it didn't happen.

After going through this process with my Creator, I realized from a very young age that I truly want to be a world changer. I hate for things to stay the same. I am an agent of change. I want to realize my full potential. I want to lead people to their Creator. I want to see lives change. I want to be known. I want to leave a legacy for my children, grandchildren, and great-grandchildren in which my ceiling becomes the floor of their life. I want people to say that my life, my journey, encouraged them on their own. I want to do something that no one has ever done before in a way that no one has done it. I want my Creator to get all the credit. I want you to read this book and begin your own journey of discovering your true identity and fulfilling your destiny.

Values

Values are strong foundational beliefs that anchor our lives. They are the things that matter most to us. They are the nonnegotiable characteristics that best describe who we are and what we live for. They are important to our souls.

Think about where you spend most of your time and effort. When are you the happiest and most fulfilled? Examine what frustrates you. Frustration can sometimes show you where your life is out of balance and how you are not making time for the very things you value. Here are some words to get you thinking about what you value:

Adventure. Authenticity. Beauty. Collaboration. Comfort. Community. Compassion. Competence. Competition. Control. Consistency. Creativity. Determination. Diligence. Efficiency. Elegance. Encouragement. Excellence. Faithfulness. Family. Freedom. Fun. Gentleness. Genuineness. Good Taste. Gracefulness. Growth. Hard Work. Harmony. Honesty. Humility. Humor. Impacting People. Independence. Influence. Integrity. Joy. Love. Laughter. Loyalty. Making Money. Marriage. Obedience. Orderliness. Organization. Patience. Peace. Perfection. Performance. Persistence. Physical Vitality. Productivity. Purity. Quality. Recognition. Relationships. Relaxation. Respect for Earth. Respect for Life. Respect for People. Responsibility. Risk-taking. Romance. Security. Self-Discipline. Self-Control. Self-Expression. Sensitivity. Service. Sexual Fulfillment. Silence. Sincerity. Solitude. Spiritual Growth. Spirituality. Stability. Success. Tolerance. Tongue-Control. Tranquility. Trust. Truth. Unity. Vision. Water-walking. Winning. Worship.

Did some of the words jump off the page at you? Highlight them, circle them, or write them down in your journal. Contemplate the *why* of them. This exercise was so difficult for me when I first attempted it. I spent most of my time staring at the words. What *did* I value? I spent so much of my life pleasing everyone else that I was not even sure what I valued, what mattered the most to me.

When I read the list again, I got hung up on picking words I *should* pick, things I believed I should value if I were a good person. Honesty. Peace. Service. Going to church. Whew! My head was spinning. Consulting my Creator was mandatory for even figuring out what I value, for what He created me to value. I discovered mine are unique to me and will lead me to my destiny. Yours will, too.

Authentic Relationships

Authentic relationships with my Creator and with the people in my life is my number one core value. I discovered I have no time for chitchat, small talk, or mindless conversations. I want to know my Creator and the people I love deeply. I want to know them and be known by them. I do not have time for anything else.

Years ago, I would have defined my values as God, family, and others—all relationships. While that is still true, I learned they must be deep and transparent. I needed relationships where I could just be me. I have been designed with a large capacity for relationships: meaningful, direct, and authentic ones. These are critical to my identity and my destiny! I need purpose in everything, even in my relationships. I discovered this is why I hate to play games. I would rather have deep, meaningful conversations instead. You may have described this value as communication. You are right. I love to talk.

Marriage and Family

I value my marriage and my family. Sounds trite, huh? Most of us would list our family as something we value—or at least we believe we should. However, the way I value them is a bit different. That is why I list them separately from authentic relationships. In my StrengthsFinder 2.0 results, I am called a maximizer. If something is good, I want it great; if it is great, I want it grand; if it is grand, I want it grandiose! I love bigger and better. Relationally, I am the same. I want more from my marriage, more from that relationship, more for and from my husband and our kids. I want us all to be better because of each other. I want my Creator to use our family to change the world. My greatest fear is that individually or collectively they will settle for less than they were created for. (Yes, I drive all of them crazy.)

Growing

My second value is all about growing and learning so I reach my full potential. Then I want to replicate, duplicate, and impart all that is within me. I hate being bored. I want to be stimulated. I want to feel alive, and through my times of intimacy with my Creator, I was shown this is an important part of my destiny—to be fully alive, growing daily, and producing "fruit" that lasts an eternity. Without consulting my Creator day by day, I do not think I would have been able to state this as a value.

At first glance, my life and past did not seem to reflect this value. I did not go to college and did not have a great deal of desire to excel when I was in school. However, my Creator reminded me that I love to read. I literally devour books. Reading is learning. I love to go to conferences. I love to listen to speakers. I love to hang out with people who are smarter than I am. And though my life choices took me from a path of structured learning, I appeased my hunger for knowledge in a more unstructured way. I long for knowledge that produces personal growth. For years now, I have asked my Creator to be my teacher, and daily I try to learn something new.

Action

I value doing something, anything—even if it is wrong. I am not scared of failure, but I am scared to death of sitting by and doing nothing. I hate sitting still. I hate being bored. I hate worrying and wringing hands. I hate problems with no answers. I like action. It is so affirming to have your Creator show you that the very thing that often drives people crazy about your personality is the very thing placed inside of you to ensure that you will fulfill your destiny! It is incredibly encouraging to know that you are created on purpose for a purpose—even if you are often misunderstood or told to sit still.

Solitude and More ...

Solitude, wide-open spaces, aesthetically pleasing environments, influencing, respect, and responsibility round out the top ten values of my life. I have others that I also try to be intentional about living from, but these are the main ones.

A Satisfied Soul

As I reviewed the words I had written about myself, I actually laughed out loud. What a complicated, complex, convoluted individual I am. What was my Creator thinking when He made me? I remember wondering that in the early days of making a careful assessment of who I was. Today, I see how uniquely I have been crafted on purpose for a purpose.

My needs, my wants, and my values have all become indicators that escorted me to my destiny and motivate me to stay on course. When those are out of balance, I stall. I get stuck. Because of this knowledge, it has given me clarity in what to say yes to and what to say no to. I can always tell when I have made choices that do not reflect my core values, needs, or wants. I become overwhelmed, irritable, and frustrated.

Aligning these three things—my needs, wants, and values—with the way I spend my time is vital to my identity and destiny. This is literally what it means to stay true to yourself. This is what it means for our souls to be healthy. Often, I need to recalibrate my schedule and make sure I am operating out of my values. I need to be kind to my soul.

What about you? Have you made a careful assessment of yourself? I encourage you to use the assessments I referenced here or chose your own.

Do you know what you need to be you? Have you assessed your wants and defined your values? If not, I encourage you to spend the time to make a careful assessment of who you are. Consult your Creator about the needs, wants, and values placed inside of you before time began and get rid of the ones that are not part of who you are. You will feel so free. You will be ready to fly on the wings of eagles and reach your destiny.

Key Chapter Concepts for Contemplation:

- Your soul can be healthy or unhealthy.
- Make a careful assessment of you; you might start liking you.
- It is your responsibility to control your emotions.
- Making a careful assessment of your needs, wants, and values is critical for a healthy soul.
- Knowing your soul allows you to make choices that line up with your identity and destiny.

CHAPTER 8

Your Eternal Identity

Your spirit is the eternal essence of you. Your spirit is the part of you that will remain when your body is gone. Your spirit knows and recognizes truth that does not need an explanation. Your spirit requires no words to communicate. Your spirit is the part of you that was known by your Creator before time began.

Our need to be known, our need to matter, to belong, and make a difference, is strong within our souls. I believe our souls ask the questions, "Who am I?" and "Why am I here?" and our spirits hold the answers to those questions. I believe before time began, our Creator planted those answers inside our spirits and waits for the questions to be asked.

There is a verse in the Bible that says, "Before I formed you in the womb I knew you, and before you were born I set you apart." When I ponder these words, I am intrigued. Before I was formed, I was known. Before I was born, I was set a part for a purpose. This concept defies logic but somewhere inside of me, deeper than my soul and the logic within my brain, I agree. I hear these words and I immediately believe; I want to believe. The belief that I am known intimately, set a part for a purpose, and created exactly right produces emotions in me that cause me to take steps that will propel me into my destiny. I reject the belief that some hold to that we are finite, expendable, and unplanned creatures. Those words to not make me feel as if I can change the world. My spirit rejects those words as truth. I must learn to trust my spirit or, as some people say, trust my gut. I think they are the same.

Spirit-Recognized Truth

Your spirit knows truth. Your spirit recognizes truth. Our Creator speaks to our spirit about *who* we are and *what* we are supposed to be doing. That is happening deep within us. That concept totally blows me away. It is just too big for my soul (my mind) to comprehend, but in my spirit, I recognize it as truth.

Let me give you an example of your spirit responding separately from you soul.

Have you ever been moved to tears over pure beauty—the beauty of an evening sunset that lit the sky up with brilliant colors or a waterfall that cascaded down the face of a mountain, spraying off a mist that was a multi-colored prism of rain? Perhaps it was when you watched your child sleeping and a smile spread across his mouth, leaving you to wonder what he was dreaming about. Maybe it was a specific melody of music or the words of a song that cut straight to the core of you by describing feelings or thoughts you recognized but could not have articulated? Was it a time that you saw pure innocence in the eyes of a child? Did your tears surprise you? Sunsets, waterfalls, music, lyrics, babies, and beauty all travel past the logic of our soul and go straight to our spirits, communicating a truth that we recognize but cannot name with mere words.

The emotions or feelings we sense here are not filtered through a belief. The scenarios go past our soul and our logic, to speak to our spirit, suggesting we are incredible creatures, more than accidents, connected to creation and others. They communicate that we are eternal beings with eternal purposes. Beauty, music and babies cause a wonder inside us that is difficult to contain or explain. When my Creator speaks to me, I feel the same way. Tears come to my eyes as my spirit recognizes truth my soul often cannot—that my Creator has a great love and a unique destiny that was planned for me before time began. I am a part of something so much bigger than myself. I need to be me. Our spirits are tuned to a different frequency. It is one of divine favor and blessings bestowed freely and lavishly. The communication is between my Creator and the essence of me. It is all so hard to explain, but my spirit alone recognizes this truth. Quickly, I must choose to believe it before my soul, my logical brain, or other human beings try to distort its melody. I choose to trust the divine dialogue going on inside of me and wooing me to my identity. Like our bodies and our souls, this part of ourselves must be given attention or we will never tap into the frequency or crack the code of our unique identity and destiny.

I would dare to say that, of our three parts, our spirits receive the least amount of our attention. Our bodies are fed daily and rightly so, because if we did not eat we would die. Our souls are constantly being fed a diet of our wants. "I want, what I want, when I want it." We are selfish creatures and have a vested interest in having our needs and wants met. However, our spirits do not demand. Our spirit, the eternal essence of who we are, longs to dialogue with our Creator in a place where we learn to recognize and trust the eternal truth about ourselves. Time must be carved from our busy lives to gaze upon the beautiful, the mystical, the grand, and the unexplained in our world. We must feast upon our Creator's words that penetrate our souls and pierce our spirits with truth. *Who am I?* our soul inquires. Our Creator responds, *You are mine. You are called beloved. You have a place to belong. You are planned, created on purpose for a purpose. You have a water-walking, giant-slaying history-making destiny. You will change the world.*

This inner dialogue with our Creator creeps past our logic and provides a peace that passes all understanding. It comes from times of solitude—which most of us run from. We must become comfortable being alone with ourselves and just our Creator. It is a place where no other person can journey with you because it is inside of you. In this place is where we first claim our identity and vow to fulfill our destiny. It is the place where we first recognize the truth about who we are and what we are created to do. It is the place where we first resolve to believe. It is where we will find our destiny.

I hope you have not grown impatient while reading the first chapters of this book. You may have chosen this book because you were anxious to find your purpose and begin changing the world. I believe you will do that. However, I am convinced you first need to be who you were created to be before you can ever do what you were created to do. There is one more chapter on your identity before I begin providing clues for your destiny.

Identity boot camp is almost over. Boot camp is designed to not only help you discover your identity but also to provide opportunities to practice and solidify it. Believing in and acting from your true identity guarantees success in your destiny. Practice does make perfect. I want your new identity to become your new core narrative. I want your belief in yourself to be strong and impenetrable. I want you to succeed in your world-changing mission.

Key Chapter Concepts to Consider:

- You are an eternal being created before time began.
- Your spirit recognizes truth that your soul may not.
- You must incorporate solitude, beauty, and music into your life to hear the dialogue of the spirit.
- Dialogue between your spirit and your Creator produces seeds of destiny in your life.
- Discovering your identity guarantees success in your destiny.

CHAPTER 9

Boot Camp Looks and Feels a Lot Like War

After reading the chapters on your identity, I trust I have convinced you that a strong and accurate sense of your identity as a unique creation is a must before you can believe and achieve your water-walking, giant-slaying, history-making destiny.

To test my experience and theories, I was discussing the topic of identity, destiny, and purpose with an army staff sergeant friend of mine before she departed for her third tour of duty in Iraq. I told her I had made a *secret* discovery about the importance of knowing your identity before fulfilling your destiny. She just laughed at my revelation. I was shocked when she told me my secret has been employed by the United States Army for years as a part of new recruit training. It is called *boot camp*.

The U.S. Army's boot camp is where a civilian recruit is transformed into a soldier.

Boot Camp

I wanted to learn everything I could about that transformation, because I had a sense it could be critical in learning to embrace my own identity and training others to embrace theirs. In great detail, my soldier friend outlined how much time, effort, and training the army spends in reinforcing a soldier's collective identity as a member of the U.S. Army before they ever divulge that soldier's destiny, what they call their mission.

During the first week of ten-week boot camp, new recruits receive hours of classroom instruction in the army's heritage, the seven core values of the U.S. Army, the code of military justice, and the soldier's creed. All of this information, combined with weeks of rigorous training, leads to their transformation.

As my staff-sergeant friend talked, I imagined a long line of new army recruits on the first day they report for duty. I can feel their nervousness as they contemplate the unknown. They are so young, probably nineteen or twenty years old—way too young, in my opinion, to sign up to defend our country and possibly go to war. This is my default, fearful mom opinion. In reality, I would be a proud mom if any of my sons enlisted in the armed forces, just as many other moms and dads have proudly watched as their sons and daughters have volunteered to fight for and protect our freedom in this country. This is a high calling and grand purpose.

These young recruits are all so different when they enlist. They fit no mold. They have diverse educations, aspirations, and experiences. They come from different family environments and histories. Yet they have all signed up for the same thing: to serve their country, to be a part of something bigger than themselves. I admire them. It takes a great deal of courage and faith just to enlist.

Do you think these young recruits actually know what they have signed up for? Do they really understand what they have committed their lives and future to? I doubt it. They may have signed up because they want to do something that has meaning and purpose. Maybe they want to be a part of something far bigger than their individual selves. They may have joined to follow family members or continue a family tradition. The reasons may vary for joining, but they all end up in the same place—boot camp. Boot camp is designed to provide these young soldiers with a collective water-walking, giant-slaying, history-making identity and destiny.

Soon after enlisting, I am sure some of these young people may question their decision or even wish they could run back home, while others are gung-ho and eager to begin their journey of purpose. Either way, by enlisting they have begun a journey of faith—faith in the U.S. Army. They have given up their individual rights and the control of their own lives for the privilege of being identified as a soldier in the

United States Army. It is an honor.

Now it is the army's responsibility to train and transform these young civilians into soldiers.

Do you think on the first day of boot camp the army distributes weapons and discloses missions to these new recruits, sending them out to the front lines with a pat on the back and a *"You can do it!"* cheer? I do not think so. These new soldiers would have no chance. If they did not get themselves killed immediately, they might succeed in getting half their unit blown up. If, on that first day of boot camp, all of those anxious, out-of-shape, untrained recruits were given battle plans without any instruction or sense of what it means to be a soldier in the U.S. Army, chaos and mayhem would ensue and most would quit or die on the first day they started.

Thus the army has a different plan, a tried and true method. It is called boot camp.

Recruits begin an intentional, intensive, and repetitive process designed to teach each new solider his or her individual and collective identity as a member of the U.S. Army. While missions are given based on assessments of individual ability, strengths, and aptitudes, the identity of a U.S. soldier is common to everyone who survives boot camp.

Do you think the army lets new recruits define or determine their own identity? Do you think the army polls each new recruit and asks, "What do you think the identity of a soldier should be?" Do they put it out for a vote? Of course not. The army, and only the army, defines the identity of its soldiers. It is constant and does not change. In both word and deed, the army begins the time-honored process of bestowing the new recruits' identity upon them. It is woven throughout the ten weeks of boot camp.

"Treat a man as he is, and he will remain as he is. Treat a man as he could be, and he will become what he should be."

– Ralph Waldo Emerson

That is what the army does. It teaches the new recruit who he or she can be.

The process cannot be rushed. The army stresses and repeats who they are and how they are expected to behave when bearing their new identity. The bar is high and the training intense for this transformation to occur.

It takes time for the army recruit to believe in and trust their new identity. The officers know it will take a while before the recruits' behavior mirrors this new identity. That is why repetition is important. The soldiers memorize and recite, out loud and often, their creed and core values to make the army's belief system and values their own.

The army knows what I have learned: If recruits believe they are U.S. Army soldiers, they will act like U.S. Army soldiers. That is why so much time and money is spent on training, on repetition, on boot camps and practice drills—to solidify their identity in such a way that when they are in the middle of their mission, they will never question who they are or what they were trained to do.

The recruit is taught to trust that training.

By the time they graduate and leave boot camp, they have become a U.S. soldier. The creed is no longer something they just recite; it is who they are and a part of them. It defines them. It is a statement of their collective identity.

The Soldier's Creed

- I am an American Soldier.
- I am a warrior and a member of a team.
- I serve the people of the United States and live the Army values.
- I will always place the mission first.
- I will never accept defeat.
- I will never quit. I will never leave a fallen comrade.
- I am disciplined, physically and mentally tough, trained and
- proficient in my warrior tasks and drills.
- I always maintain my arms, my equipment and

myself.

- I am an expert and I am a professional.
- I stand ready to deploy, engage, and destroy the enemies of the United States of America in close combat.
- I am a guardian of freedom and the American way of life.
- I am an American Soldier.

Notice the creed has many sentences beginning with *I am*. Those are the identity sentences stressing who they are. The other sentences tend to begin with *I will*. Those sentences reflect the behaviors they have chosen to demonstrate in advance of their circumstances, in advance of being given their mission.

I felt like one of those eager, untrained, clueless young recruits when I first said yes to being who I was created to be and fulfilling my destiny. Like them, I had no idea what I had signed up for. I had no idea my life was not my own. I had enlisted for a mission of purpose, not knowing where it would lead or the training it would require. I was both scared and excited. However, although I said yes, I was in no way ready for my Creator to reveal His plans for me, because I was struggling to grasp and act out of my new identity. If I had known what my destiny would entail before fully coming to terms with my true identity, I would have fallen on the floor in laughter. If I would have seen the battles I have been required to fight, I might have quit before I started or turned tail and run for the hills.

In the beginning stages, just like our new army recruit, I had not yet embraced my true identity. I was more comfortable with who I was instead of who I was created to be. My past looked like it disqualified me from a future of divine purpose. I had no obvious talents. I talked too much, listened too little, and spoke with a Southern accent while frequently butchering the English language. I write like I talk, I hate to leave home, and I have no college degree. I been divorced, despise math, and am frightened to death to try anything I am not good at. When I looked at me through my own eyes, I did not see much potential; my identity screamed mediocrity. Like our young army recruits, I needed to go through an identity boot camp if I was ever going to be who I was created to be, and you will need to do the same.

My Personal Creed

Chapters of this book were designed to be—the beginning of your identity boot camp. To end the first half of this book, I would like to share with you a creed I wrote for myself, inspired by the Soldier's Creed. I decided I needed a creed of my own. One that stated who I was and what I was willing to do. I needed a powerful statement of identity that I could repeat often to myself when doubt crept in. So I wrote the following. Feel free to borrow it or, even better, consult your Creator and write your own.

I am a beloved child of God.
I am lavished with love.
I am fearfully and wonderfully made.
I am a masterpiece woven together by God in my mother's womb.
But even before that, I was imagined and crafted by the God of the universe on purpose for a purpose.
Good plans have been designed especially for me.
I have a destiny that will transform lives, change history, and answers prayers.
I am a child of God.
I embrace that identity. I trust in that identity.
I will not allow anyone else to ever tell me who I am, except my Maker.
I will only consult my Creator for my identity and my destiny.
I am a water walker, giant slayer, and history maker.
I refuse to quit.
I will change the world.
I will have the courage to be me.

The path to your purpose requires you to embrace your identity. It must be unshakeable. No more self-doubt or low self-esteem. Going through boot camp will make your identity stick. It is designed to make you ready for your water-walking, giant-slaying, history-making destiny.

You need to know that you can trust yourself when the battles come. Trust me, they will come. You need to trust that when things get tough, you will not quit. Your boot camp was also designed to test your faith in your Creator. Having said that, I must warn you that on some days, your boot camp will look and feel a lot like war!

Deep Trust

I have to tell you a secret: No one feels qualified to do what they are created and called to do. I certainly do not on many days. I still feel like the poster child for ordinary. Boot camp is difficult, but it is a necessary precursor to receiving our marching orders. It is there where we are prepared for our purpose. It makes us better and it makes us stronger. It establishes and reinforces our belief in our identity, but it also does so much more. Boot camp establishes a deeper trust between you and your Commander.

When my oldest son Austin was in the fourth grade, I was asked to teach his Sunday school class. The lesson that day was on trusting our Creator. I wondered all week how to illustrate this lesson in a way that rowdy fourth grade boys could embrace. I read through several inspirational books and pondered several ideas before tossing them out. At the very last minute, I received divine inspiration.

When the boys all arrived to class and finally got settled in their chairs, I asked them to come up and form a line in front of me. I asked Austin to go last. One by one, I asked the boys to come stand about two feet in front of me, with his back to me. I then asked the first boy to close his eyes and cross his hands over his chest.

Then I told him to fall backward.

His eyes flew open and he turned around, shocked. I repeated the instructions, got him in place again, told him to close his eyes and again said, "Fall backward."

He could not do it.

Hands flew up, and all fifteen of the other fourth grade boys screamed, "Let me!" bravely adding, "I can do it!"

But they also could not.

Not a one, except for my son.

Confidently, he stood in front of me, back turned, eyes closed, and arms crossed, and with complete trust he fell back into my arms without hesitation. All the boys cheered. He smiled. He was able to do what the others could not do because he *knew* me. He had experiences with me in which I had been faithful. He had a history and a relationship with me, thus he was able to completely trust me.

Trust cannot be rushed. It is evidence-based. It is established through experience; you could say it is a boot camp-like experience. We learn to trust another person, or even a product, over time. Trust is birthed from a history of faithfulness. Trust is a peace that settles in our soul and originates from a deep, intimate relationship or knowledge of another. Trust is achieved slowly during the routine daily dialogue of our lives.

The more trust that has been established between two individuals, the more the other person is invited to speak into our lives and our circumstances. In order to follow another, trust must be built. That trust is built when someone consistently follows through what he or she has said.

Military boot camp exercises and drills are designed for the purpose of establishing and cementing trust between peers and those in authority. Trusting that leaders will do what they say and provide the resources needed to fulfill the mission is critical to success. Boot camp shows us whom we can trust. And it also teaches us to trust ourselves and our training. God's boot camp is no different.

In our lives, we go through boot camp situations that are beyond our ability to fix and will require divine intervention. It seems delayed answers to prayers, unexpected circumstances, and problems with no immediate solutions are all exercises and drills used by our Maker to ascertain our level of faith and trust in His leadership and our new identity.

We are competent people. We get up, go to work, earn a paycheck, and then drive the car we bought with our hard-earned money to the local store to buy groceries so we can feed ourselves. We like being independent, problem-solving people. All of these actions are done without any outside help, we proudly claim. On any given day, we human beings can fight fires, save lives, get an education, buy a home, get a job, build a house, paint a picture, invent a device, and have a baby all without divine intervention. We are wonderfully and fearfully made. However, if we are to attempt world-changing destinies, we are going to have to tap into the divine. We will need to be trained in how and when to attempt the impossible. That is why we need to go through boot camp—to learn to trust our identity, others, and our Creator.

Words in My Spirit

Start an international organization to help people find their purpose. Copyright all the materials. You will travel the world. I will give you the financial resources equivalent to Starbucks. You will meet the needs of those in society that no one is meeting. You will build them homes. You will call the family. You will have daughters. You will start Courage Cafés. You will hire the best of the best and pay them marketplace salaries. You will united as one. You will be of one heart, one mind, and one spirit. You will write a book. You will speak to stadiums full of people. Your children, the next generation, will take the organization to places you cannot dream of.

All of those words have been whispered to my spirit. Some have come true and others I am still believing for. When I first heard them, I was filled with a wonder and excitement that is difficult to articulate. I had spent so much time cementing my identity that when the words of my destiny were finally revealed, I was overwhelmed by my assignment. While my soul and my logical brain knew I could never attempt to fulfill these on my own, my spirit recognized that this was exactly what I was created to do. I was humbled for that which I was chosen and prepared. My entire life made sense as those words settled deep within my soul.

When I received my mission, I was reeling so much from a very intensive boot camp experience that I did not realize at the time was designed to solidify my identity and prepare me for this very destiny. All I knew was that boot camp felt a lot like war. On some days, I could not tell the difference. However, when my mission was revealed, I realized my circumstances were ordained by my Maker to prepare me for the future. Through those difficult experiences, I gained a new level of trust in myself and in my Creator. How thankful I am for them all. I am still drawing encouragement from them today. Boot camp taught me to trust myself and my Creator at a whole new level.

To fulfill the world-changing destiny assigned to you, you must have complete trust in yourself and your Creator. You must have complete trust that you are prepared for your purpose. You must have complete trust that provision of resources will be there for you to succeed. In addition, you must earn the trust of your Maker. He must know that you can be trusted to finish the task He assigns and not to quit when things get tough.

Boot Camp Weeds Out Quitters

You have to resolve within yourself, before you ever start on this journey of purpose, that quitting is not an option. I often play mind games with myself to bring clarity to situations. I treat every obstacle, every problem, and every opportunity in my life as either a test to be won or a battle to be fought. Both situations require my commitment to the calling and purpose on my life. Both require that I not quit when things get tough.

The situation that is a test is designed by my Creator to teach me, test me, or strengthen me while the other is a battle designed to take something from me that is rightfully mine. The first, I want to pass, to win, or to succeed, because I know the lesson is required to move me into the strategic position designed for me. It shows what is best for me and fully prepares me for future trials and circumstances. The lesson makes me strong. It teaches me to fight so I am competent and deadly in battle. I want to prove that I will not quit and that I can be depended upon.

The other battle— The other situation that is trying to rob me is a battle that puts steel one that puts steel in my spine, makes me angry, and causes me to fight for and take back what is rightfully mine. I feel much stronger when I see myself as a warrior in battle rather than a victim of my circumstances. Through boot camp and war-like situations, I have been trained to fight. I am confident. I am prepared to face my enemy. I have been guaranteed victory. I will not quit.

In both of these scenarios, I must resolve not to quit when things get difficult. There is much at stake, and I have come to realize that my part is critical to what happens in my world. One of my greatest fears is to realize that I was a day away from victory or promotion but I gave up and quit one day too soon.

Everything can change in a single day. What if tomorrow is the day everything changes? What if you quit too soon?

Boot camp weeds out the quitters. Before you are given the details of your destiny, you will be put through rigorous situations, war-like circumstances, to determine if you will quit or not. Boot camp has taught me that winning simply means not quitting. During some of the most difficult days of my life, the only prayer I could utter—through clenched teeth and with tears running down my cheeks—was, "*I will not quit!*" I have resolved, made up my mind in advance, that no matter the test I have been given or the battle I am fighting, I will not quit. What about you? Say it with me: ***I will not quit.***

Obey Without Question

In the military, there are clear lines of authority. You learn immediately to say, "Yes sir!" and not question commands or orders given by your superiors.

There is an extreme level of trust that is required to obey without question. Without that level of trust, a situation can become abusive and destructive. As we talked about previously, boot camp is designed to build that level of trust.

In the family I was raised in, it was exactly the same way. My dad was the head of the household. There were no majority votes or soliciting of opinions. Everything worked well if we just did what we were told. Now, my dad was not abusive. He was not a dictator. Repeatedly, he had demonstrated his love for his family, his integrity, and his ability to provide for us. He had a vision for our family and we all had important parts, but at critical and stressful times he had to know he could depend upon our instant obedience. We were able to do that because we had complete trust in him. Because of his character and love, obeying was easy, even if I didn't have all of my *why* questions answered.

I believe our Creator requires the same of us, if we are to be and do all that our destiny requires.

One morning, I felt these words penetrate to the core of my being: "Sell your house."

What? Are we moving? I thought.

Silence followed. It was decision time for me: Do I obey what I have come to trust and what I have learned is the direction of my Creator? After much discussion with my husband and family, we decided to "step out in faith" even though we did not know where we were moving to or what we were supposed to do. Yes, people thought we were crazy. Even I thought so on some days. However, we did as ordered *without* having all our desired answers.

When my husband gave his blessing—it took two weeks for him to wrap his brain around all of this—I then called a realtor who put the house on the market. It sold in a week. I resigned from my volunteer positions at church and school, told all our family and friends, informed my pastor, and began packing boxes—all without having any idea where we were going. I had children in elementary and middle school at the time. I had no idea where they would be in school the following year. It was June. I figured I had three months until it was an issue.

People asked me over and over, "Where are you moving?"

I said, "I have no idea." I continued to pack and prepare to move until I received additional orders.

I could do all of this because I had gone through boot camp. I had proved I could be trusted, and I knew that my Creator could be trusted as well. I had complete faith that my family and I were being strategically moved to where we were supposed to be. I knew this was an exercise in obedience. Would I obey without having all the answers? Now that trust was being put to the test. It was a test I desperately wanted to pass, and I truly believe my destiny hinged on it.

Weeks later, after the house was sold, the moving van ordered, and the last boxes packed, I was given an address through divine provision. I was delirious. We were moving! I felt I had just received my marching orders and was heading straight into my long-awaited destiny. Are you in a situation where you do not have all the answers but sense your spirit is leading you on a journey of faith? It a test or a war. Before you act, you need to decide if you are being fired upon by the enemy or if it is friendly fire.

You Are in a War

News flash. There is a war being fought over you and your destiny. God's boot camp and subsequent tests are designed to prepare you. However, to fulfill your purpose you will be required to fight for your life.

Boot camp teaches you how to respond when you are in that battle.

When you are being fired upon, take cover immediately. Then take a tactical pause. Be still and do nothing. Then you must ascertain if the fire is enemy or friendly. If it is enemy fire, you give them all you got. Fire away and call for reinforcements. However, if it is friendly fire, stay put and do nothing until it is over.

"What? I'm going to be shot at by friends?" I said aloud.

This was probably the hardest lesson I have had to learn. I expected to be shot at by the "bad guys," but not by the good ones. I guess what I found even more surprising than being shot at with "friendly fire" was being betrayed by those I thought were on my team. I am not going to spend an enormous amount of time on this topic except to say this really happened. I have experienced it, and so will you in your journey of purpose. You will be betrayed. Expect it. Train for it. Prepare for it. The army does.

You do not respond to friendly fire the way you do enemy fire. When you have determined that you are being fired upon by the good guys, take cover and do not fire back. That means keep your mouth shut. Go underground. Wait until it stops. Do not hunt them down or murder them with your mouth. Take a tactical pause. Determine who is still loyal to you and the mission, and stay loyal to them. Regroup. Reassign positions if necessary. Then get back to work. Friendly fire is a part of war.

I wish someone would have told or taught me this lesson early in my boot camp. It was a lesson I learned much later. I learned the hard way that it is wise to be slow in letting people be members of a team or giving them pieces of your heart. As we discussed earlier, trust is built over time. *People must earn trust.* When they do, then they are given more responsibilities. This is the way the army does it. You advance through a series of well-defined job responsibilities and roles. Promotions occur when you have shown yourself to be capable and trustworthy. It would be wise to do the same. Promoting people into the inner circle of our hearts and lives should occur only as they prove trustworthy.

I let people into my heart, my life, my home, and the non-profit I founded very easily. I am extremely naïve and trusting, thus it is extremely upsetting to me when I am fired upon or betrayed by friends. I spend an enormous amount of time expending energy into conversations that take place only in my head, instead of holding people accountable for their actions. I give grace and second chances, only to be fired upon again. My strength is my weakness. I believe in people. I am inclusive. I see potential. I invest a lot in my relationships. It is hard for me to let go and leave people to their own choices.

In one of my boot camp experiences involving friendly fire, I took a tactical pause. I felt like I had been shot in the back. As I whined about the situation, these words came to my mind: *If it is so hard for you to let people go, then be slower at letting them in.*

I can do that? It is not mean?

Somewhere in my Southern and Christian upbringing, I thought you had to let everyone into your life and inner circle. I now realize that is not necessarily true. Trusting the wrong people can lead to betrayal and friendly fire.

Fighting friendly fire with a tactical pause and silence are the best *weapons* to use. Without them, you can easily be derailed from fulfilling your destiny. To minimize these types of attacks, you need to use wisdom and seek discernment about adding people to your life. Before giving them access to your home, your heart, your family, and the destiny you are fulfilling, you must do all you can to find out if they are trustworthy. Do background checks, talk to those with whom they have worked for or worked with, and do not be afraid to do your due diligence. If the individual is offended, that should be considered a red flag. Here are three simple things to keep in mind that are of great help:

- Go slow.
- "Hear" from your Creator.
- Guard your heart.

While we cannot judge a person's heart, we can judge their fruit. So be careful. Watch out for friendly fire. Their purpose is to stall your plans and make you quit. When you learn to use your weapons, you will be unstoppable. Always keep in mind that "friendly fire" is a part of your boot camp to train and prepare you to fulfill your destiny. When your training is complete, you will be a fierce warrior!

Depend Upon a "Battle Buddy"

Boot camp trains you to be the best you that you can possibly be, but it also teaches that you cannot complete your mission all alone. We must depend upon others for success.

It is okay not to have all of the answers. We need to be okay with that truth. Answers can come through others, to us directly, and through the process of waiting. Yes, I said waiting. I hate to wait. It is very hard for me. When I began to understand the details of my destiny, all I wanted to know was *how* it was going to happen. I spent hours and hours wondering, planning, and agonizing over the *how*. It is quite humbling to realize that alone I do not have all the answers I need. Waiting is an exercise in trust. As we pause to exhibit patience, it allows us the space to listen to others, our own heart, and our Creator for important details of our battle plan.

Relax. Take it day by day or even hour by hour if you do not have all the answers. Try to view your present circumstances through the lens of boot camp. Embrace the training that is required for water-walking, giant-slaying, history-making destinies. Reach out to a buddy.

There is one more benefit of boot camp—one I learned from a retired veteran. He had tears in his eyes when he shook my hand after a Sunday evening service, and he thanked me for the encouragement I had tried to give from the stage. I was talking about the purpose of boot camp. He told me I was right but that I had left out the most important thing you receive in boot camp—a battle buddy. He continued, "The guys I went through boot camp with, and the ones I continued to fight beside to execute our missions, were the closest relationships I have had in my life, outside my wife and children. When you train with someone, fight with them, and believe in a mission that is bigger than yourself, it binds you together in a way nothing else can. Some of those men are gone now and some I have not seen in over thirty years, but I will never forget the influence and impact they had on my life and our mission."

Well said, my new friend. A battle buddy is someone that goes through boot camp with you, someone who holds you accountable, encourages you not to quit, and believes in the mission that you would both sacrifice your time, your talent, your treasure, and even your life for.

I, too, have experienced those relationships and know that without them I would have quit a long time ago. When you come to grips with your water-walking, giant-slaying, history-making destiny, you will be graciously surrounded with very strategic people and relationships—ones that will sustain, nourish, and support you during the difficult days of boot camp and through the dangers of war. These relationships are ones that you will be grateful for all your life. They become a part of you, even if you have not seen or talked to these people for years.

When Hurricane Katrina hit the Mississippi Gulf Coast and New Orleans, Louisiana area in 2005, my heart broke. Mississippi is my home state. I was moved not only with compassion, but also with a great desire toward action. I immediately volunteered to go with a group from San Carlos, California to do relief work.

When we began preparations for the trip, we were a group of strangers. By the time we returned home from our mutual experience ten days later, we were lifelong friends, bonded by an experience that is difficult to describe unless you were there to participate in it with us. It was difficult and, at the same time, immensely satisfying. Together we made a difference. Together we did more than we ever could have done alone.

The army is intentional about putting a young new recruit with other recruits who are starting out in the same place as they discover their identity prior to embarking on their mission. This common journey is an incredible bonding process. It is true that "we are better together."

Better Together

I can hear some of you asking, "*Why?*" There are three main reasons:

☐ *Big, impossible, life-changing, world-altering, incredible purposes and missions cannot be accomplished alone.*

There is a power that multiplies whenever human beings collectively agree on anything, whether good or bad—it is the power to do the impossible.

Our team at Courage Worldwide has lived this truth firsthand. We all agree it is wrong for a child to be sold for sex. It is our common language. Because of that common belief and our core value and emphasis on unity, we believe that we can do what some would call impossible. We believe we can build a home, a Courage House, for victims of sex trafficking in every city in the world that needs one. We believe we can engage a million people to build a thousand homes in a hundred countries during the next ten years so that hundreds of thousands of children can be rescued, restored, and told the truth that they too were created on purpose for a purpose.

Every day, five or six days a week, for hours a day, we work toward this common goal, speaking the same language, engaged in the impossible. These individuals that I have the honor of working with at Courage Worldwide are my family, my battle buddies, and my fellow warriors. They have my back and I have theirs. Without them, I could not do what I am created to do. Together we are able to accomplish more, faster, than any of us could alone. Our collective power, energy, and creativity astound even us, but we have been brought together using our unique purposes to further an eternal purpose. Wow, What an honor to be a part of a team like this!

☐ *You have an enemy, an enemy who wants you to fail at accomplishing your purpose and your mission.*

Your enemy knows that if you ever realize your true identity, then your chance of success in your destiny increases. The enemy will attack you very early and frequently when you embark on a journey of purpose. Your finances, relationships, and health will all be attacked. These attacks are designed to distract you, make you forget who you are, why you are fighting, and what the mission is. You need to be reminded by other people. You are going to need courage, but you are also going to need somebody to watch your back. It is much easier to *take courage* when you are surrounded by others with weapons. Your battle buddies stand with you when you are fighting. They have resources and experiences that you do not. Because they are not emotionally involved in the battles that are personal to you, it is easier for them to encourage and support you in your situation when you just can't.

☐ *Small groups forge bonds that allow members to see in us what we cannot see in ourselves.*

We all need someone to believe in us, cheer for us, and kick us in the butt when we need it. Our battle buddies do this for us. I find it fascinating that the people I work and serve with see my potential much easier than I do. They encourage me when I get down. They pursue me when I doubt. They challenge me when I am tempted to give up, and they love me even when I fail. They help me "change the world," and your battle buddies will too.

When a group discovers that its collective identity and destiny is more powerful than the members' own individual ones, they will accomplish more than they dared to ask or imagine. They will literally change the world around them. While doing this work and pursuing the impossible, there is a bond forged that is extremely strong and rarely broken. I am so thankful for the encouragement and company of those who are called to the same mission I am. I cannot imagine doing what I do without them. They make me better.

"I will attempt something so great that it is doomed to fail unless God be in it."

~ John Haggai

These words are my personal motto and heart's desire.

Ready for Your Mission

Boot camp. Rigorous training, both physical and mental, is required to prepare army recruits and us for our grand purposes. It cannot be avoided, diminished, or rushed. Oh, how I wish it could.

The days, months, and—yes—even years of boot camp can seem long and often uneventful, but be encouraged! You are being prepared for action; your time is coming. During this arduous process of preparation, something amazing will or may have already transpired. It is difficult to detect at first. But wait for it. It is worth it, I promise.

You see, somewhere along the way, the forced training and discipline start to become a habit instead of a chore. Our bodies, minds, and emotions begin to reflect the identity and training that has been bestowed and inflicted upon us. We see evidence of our new identity—evidence of who we were meant to be. At that point, our behaviors begin to betray our belief. Just like a young army recruit, we begin to act out our true identity!

Now you are ready for your mission. You are finally ready to hear and believe what was planned for you before time began. Not only that, but because of the new confidence in your identity, you will actually start to believe that, partnered with your Creator and your battle buddies, you can accomplish the impossible: the mission assigned to you.

You now begin to understand for the first time that **who you are** has a direct correlation to **what you are to do.**

Not just anyone can do what you have been assigned to do. It is your very own unique purpose.

I end this section as we began it ...

Before time began, you were created on purpose for a purpose.

Now that you know your identity, you can be released into your water-walking, giant-slaying, history-making destiny!

Key Chapter Concepts to Consider

1. Boot camp can feel a lot like war.

2. You must be trained to trust your identity.

3. You will need a battle buddy.

4. Expect friendly fire.

5. Treat every situation as a test to pass or a battle to be won.

PART TWO

Your Destiny

CHAPTER 10

From the Possible to the Impossible

Congratulations! You made it through identity boot camp. I pray you are daily embracing your identity as a child of God, confident that your Creator will lead you in the path He has chosen for you. Keep those five-by-seven cards nearby. You will need your new vocabulary to silence the negative tape that has been playing in your mind for years. Silence it with truth. Do not be surprised or discouraged when your new identify is challenged as your embark upon your journey of discovering and fulfilling your water-walking, giant-slaying, history-making destiny. Now that you know *who you are*, it is time to ask *what am I supposed to be doing?*

The answer is: (drumroll please)—the impossible.

That is right. You were created to do the impossible. That is why this entire journey requires courage. When the details of your destiny are revealed to you by your Creator, your first instinct will be to scream, *"That's impossible!"* You are right. Alone, your destiny is impossible. Your destiny requires that you leave your comfort zones for the unknown.

"We must leave the human boundaries that define our lives and step into a journey of total dependence on God's perspective and commands; where He invades the impossible."

– Bill Johnson, *Face to Face with God*

Your mission is not safe. Some would call it impossible.

All of the thought, all of the planning that went into creating you was not so you could cruise through life sleeping on high-thread-count sheets and eating bonbons. You were created for great exploits. You were created to change the world.

However, a transition must first take place.

Into the Unknown

Yes, you were created to walk on water, slay giants with pebbles, and change the course of history. But you will not get there by being comfortable or by playing it safe. Water-walking, giant-slaying, history-making destinies are found squarely in the midst of the unknown. There is rarely a strategic plan or well-marked road map. Sadly, few have dared to venture there. The journey is by faith. The destination is unfamiliar. And the voyage is extremely uncomfortable—especially in the beginning.

Still, you have to go. You now know who you are—your true identity has been cemented in your soul. being cemented in your soul. I am certain you are restless to do something, the something only you can do. Navigating from the known to the unknown, from the boat to the water, from the possible to the impossible, is the only way. It is challenging, awkward, and even a little dangerous. However, before you can receive the details of your destiny, you must make this transition. You must learn to get comfortable being uncomfortable.

You must get out of your proverbial boat.

Have you ever tried to get out of a boat when it is sitting on the water? If you have, you know there is simply no graceful way to do it. *Picture it with me.* You have one foot in the relatively solid surface of the boat while at the same time you are looking for another fixed surface (like a dock) to place your other foot.

An exchange must take place before you can lift your body out of the boat. Of course, the boat will not be still. Your body and the boat are in constant motion as the boat pitches back and forth in the water. You feel unstable and lack confidence in your ability to make the transition at all—much less make it gracefully. You long for a hand to hold. The entire process is precarious. Now imagine this same transition going from the boat to walking on the water. "Impossible!" our minds scream. When we hear that word, we remain where we are—comfortable, yet longing and restless for more.

I have to admit, while I long for more, I like my comfort zones —I worked hard for them. I wrestle with the idea of the unknown. No one likes being tossed to and fro by waves of uncertainty. I like to feel confident, doing things I know how to do. When things are good, I want them to stay that way forever. Of course, this has not been my life experience. Over time, we all learn that nothing stays the same. Change is inevitable. And it is also necessary. Why? Change transitions us from our comfort zones to the unknown and is often the very impetus our Creator uses to move us from where we are to where He wants us to be.

That is the only reason I am a willing participant in the transition process: I want to change the world.

However, I would really like a detailed, strategic plan listing tangible steps to my destiny along with an implementation timeline. Instead I just sense a whisper—a divine invitation to leave all I know. I am scared to death, but am also reassured by my Creator that I can face and overcome my fears, my "what ifs," and my insecurities one step at a time. My deepest desire to be and do everything for which I am created, stirs and churns within me. My heart aches to do the impossible, even if it means leaving the place that I love.

Participating in the Transition

One of my most challenging transitions began on an ordinary day. I sat reading my Bible in my flower garden, my dog Jake sleeping at my feet. As I read the ancient text, I sensed the approach of change. I had been extremely comfortable for a long time, but on that day trouble brewed in my paradise. I was searching for answers to a problem that was too big for me to solve. The story I read of Abram and his nephew Lot mirrored my own. They were experiencing *strife*.

Strife? That was it! That was what I was feeling. My husband, Michael, and I were experiencing intense strife. We own an energy consulting business. Energy consulting is much like riding a roller coaster with no seat belt. Natural gas prices fluctuate minute by minute. One day you can be riding waves of profit and the next day be drowning in a sea of debt. We were experiencing the latter. We owed more money than we had in our bank account and it was due *now*. That qualifies as strife. It was extremely uncomfortable and terrifying. And it was the very thing my Creator would use to transition us from where we were to where we were supposed to be.

We had tried everything we could think of to keep from drowning in the debt we faced. This financial crisis threatened to swallow us and everything we had worked so hard for. We cashed in our 401(k)s and our kids' college funds. We sought out a bankruptcy attorney who told us bankruptcy would not provide cover or protection for our unique situation. Friends graciously loaned and gifted us money, which was a very humbling experience. Did I mention I was way out of my comfort zone and how impossible it all seemed?

The unknown loomed. I had no idea what to do. So I prayed for courage. I embraced my identity as a child of God, believing impossible would become possible.

I wrote a personal vow inspired by page 2,035 in my Bible. *Against all hope, and in spite of my circumstances, I will choose to believe. I will not waver with unbelief, because I know my Creator has the power to do what is promised even in the midst of the unknown.* There on the same page, I had written myself a note during a previous time of struggle with change and transition:

When we believe, an exchange takes place in heaven and our situation is about to change—hold on!

I was holding on tight.

Strife and fear is not good. It is paralyzing. *What should I do?* I wondered. Courage is action in spite of the fear, so what action should I take that will courageously propel me out of this mess into my destiny?

Sell your house.

What?

Sell my house? Confusion flooded my thoughts. Although our financial situation was bleak, I had the childlike faith it would change. I loved my life, my home. Even though we were going through strife, I did not want to leave. I was room-mom at my kids' school. Both my husband and I worked from home. I was on staff at our church. I had started a non-profit organization with some friends called Courage to Be You, Inc., to help people find their purpose. I had conquered my fear of public speaking and was shouting the life-changing message from a stage—and to anyone who would listen—that they were created on purpose for a purpose. I thought I was finally doing all I was created for, and for the first time in my life I felt fully alive.

To make things even sweeter, I loved my husband, Michael, more than I had on the day I married him, and I was confident he loved me just as much. My little boys were doing well in school, and my oldest son had become a fine young man of whom I was so very proud. We had amazing friends that felt more like family.

Leaving was not on my radar. Leaving was not my plan. I did not want to transition to another place.

However, the financial storm had hit. Waves of debt crashed over us while the strife weighed us down. Though my faith was strong, I was terrified of going bankrupt or being sued by our clients. The waves were so high. I was sure we would drown. However, there, in the midst of the tempest, a hand was offered to steady me. Change loomed. Transition beckoned. An invitation was offered. It just was not what I planned or wanted at the time.

Sell my house? My *home*? *Go where?* I wondered.

I had a divine invitation but no answers. Would I trust the still small voice inside of me? I had much to ponder and process. I took a long walk out in the wide open spaces. I had much to ponder and process.

After much thought and prayer, I knew the answer. We had to step out in faith—sell our home, take the equity to save our business, and move somewhere yet to be disclosed. However, still I struggled to say yes. I loved my home, my neighborhood, and the life we had built there. Michael and I had moved from Mississippi to the San Francisco Bay Area the day after we married. We lived there for fourteen years;

eight of those years were spent in the house we were now asked to give up. My *home*. The known for the unknown.

Memories flooded my thoughts as I entertained a move. Small, intimate family Christmases, loud Thanksgivings, supper clubs, late-night tuck-ins and early morning snuggles, birthday parties, girlfriend groups, bouncy houses, waiting up late for teenagers, sending children off to first grade and to college, then welcoming them home again. Our friends who became our California family. There had been so much love and laughter in that place. I had believed I would grow old there, loving my husband long after the kids had gone, waiting to greet grandbabies.

Yet I believed we had received a divine invitation to sell our home and pack up everything we owned with no idea where we would go. Was I losing my mind? No.

As I contemplated the unknown, I was reminded how very restless I had become in my very comfortable life—before the strife. The things I once had a passion for had become routine and mundane. I sensed that a new dream, one bigger than I could imagine, was about to be birthed. Writing a book, speaking to thousands, traveling the world, opening homes for people who needed them—it all seemed and sounded so impossible, especially in light of my circumstances. However, I believed it all. I had assumed I would be doing all of it from my home in the San Francisco Bay Area. Change was coming. But I did not think it would be as drastic as a new address.

I wept as I contemplated the dream that was revealed to me. I wanted it all. I had many questions, but I also had my answer.

Yes, we would go.

But what would Michael say? Would he think I was crazy? Probably. One evening, I explained to him the divine invitation that had been whispered to my spirit. Let's just say he did not see it as a divine invitation and he certainly did not embrace the idea of selling our home without knowing where we were going. Though I could understand his reluctance, I was confused. I truly believed this was what we were supposed to do, but my husband could not see it. For two weeks, I fretted and prayed. Then one morning Michael said,

"Okay, let's do it."

I was strangely excited, though I lacked answers to where we were moving.. I hired a realtor and quickly put the house up for sale, even though we still had no idea where we were going. Our friends and family thought we were scared, crazy, or running from our problems. They were wrong. We were preparing to walk on water. I wanted to do it well. I wanted the transition to be grace filled.

Our house sold in just one week—at the height of the market, before the housing collapse in 2007. We had thirty days to pack, move, enroll our kids in school, and start our new life. Yet we still had no idea where we were going. However, I was confident this transition would lead to my destiny. And it did!

CHAPTER 11

Secrets to Successful Transitions

I have learned a few secrets from my many transitions, but especially from this one. If you are willing to embrace them, you too can make the move from the known to the unknown gracefully and successfully. If the transition is one that will lead you to your water-walking, giant-slaying, history-making destiny, then it will start with a divine invitation sent directly to your heart from your Creator. That is the first secret. However, it is a challenge to determine whether the invitation is truly divine or if it is simply a desperate human attempt to fulfill your own dreams or solve your own problems.

In my experience, a divine invitation is much crazier and more risky than anything I can come up with on my own. My dreams, ideas, and solutions tend to be logical. They have a safety net or savings account attached to them and are very much something I can do within my own power and personality.

If the invitation is indeed divine, it will scare you to death. It will seem impossible.

Initially you will feel as if you cannot do it, while at the same time you will long to try. Over time, as the idea settles deep within you, you will *want* to do it. You will then dare to believe you *can* do it. The invitation will feel so right, yet at the same time you will be reluctant to leave all you know.

Waiting for a divine invitation is a must. However, I did it wrong for so long. I did it my way. I happen to be a very capable person. I am a problem solver, and I make decisions quickly and confidently.

However, when faced with situations beyond my control and much bigger than my resources, I tend to become paralyzed. That is what fear does to you—it stops you dead in your tracks. It is hard to even think or pray. After paralyzing fear, comes reactive panic. Panic makes you feel you must do something—anything—even if it is the wrong thing. You believe doing something is better than doing nothing. Your response becomes a frantic reaction. It rarely proves wise.

Been there. Done that.

I lived the first forty years of my life reacting to whatever life threw my way, taking matters into my own hands without consulting my Creator. Coming up with my own desperate solutions. That is not a recipe for a successful water-walking destiny.

There is a better way - saying yes to a divine invitation.

The Better Way

When you sense a divine invitation from your Creator to leave your comfort zone for the unknown, when you sense change or transition is coming, you have to ask the hard questions, process your feelings and fears, and then seek the advice of other people experienced in grace-filled transitions. After you have done that, take all of your thoughts, observations, feelings, questions, and doubts and write them down in a journal, unedited. This will help you untangle your feelings from the facts. It will help you discern if you are sensing a truly divine invitation from your Maker.

If it is, do not hesitate. Get out of the boat. Jump in!

While there certainly is a time to pause and ponder, I have that found divine invitations do not last forever. I do not want to miss the boat or worse, have my boat tipped over and be thrown head first into the deep end. Though I may be scared to death of leaving my comfort zones, I am more afraid of missing what I am designed to be, to see, and to do. I want to experience it all. Don't you?

To ensure I do not miss divine opportunities, I began intentionally studying successful water-walkers and their transitions from the known to the unknown. One of my favorite studies is the life of Peter, a fisherman turned fisher of men, and the original water walker. How I would love to interview him and ask him these questions:

- Why were you the only one to get out of the boat—a place you were very comfortable?
- How did you conquer your fear?
- Where did you find the courage?
- Would you do it again?
- What was going through your mind?
- Did anyone encourage you to do it?

These questions could be asked of anyone pursuing their world-changing destiny. However, in my life I could not find many flesh-and-blood people doing just that. Peter inspired me. An ordinary man who craved the impossible. He seemed to wrestle with the tension of wanting to be safe but at the same time wanting to walk on water. It seemed he knew the secret; without a divine invitation, he would literally drown.

Before you jump headfirst into the waves of the unknown, pause long enough to confirm there is a divine invitation. Start with a long, honest prayer between you and your Creator. Talk with other water walkers you know, and if you cannot find many in your own life, then study the pages of the Bible or other biographies of those who dared to leave the known for the unknown. Journal your thoughts. While a divine invitation will give rise to fear, you will also feel a rightness and excitement that gives you the courage to move out of your boat of comfort and begin considering the impossible possible.

Divine invitations are a must for successful, grace-filled transitions.

A Healthy Fear

Successful transitions require that we fear God. When I was young, I thought that fearing God meant I was supposed to be afraid of Him, but I never was. My view of God was largely shaped by my dad, who loved me madly. I assumed God did too. My dad was a strict and consistent disciplinarian but only punished me when I deserved it, like when I was being blatantly disobedient. It seemed to my little girl's mind that God followed the same pattern as my dad—loving me madly and disciplining me as warranted by my actions. Thus I tried very hard to be a good girl. I was scared to death to get in trouble and hated disappointing anyone.

My dad loves to tell the story of one of my only spanking. I was five years old, and my brother and I had been talking during what we called big church. I always had a hard time sitting still and being quiet. Even now, whispering is still difficult for me to curtail. My dad leaned over during the service and gave us *the look*. We knew he meant business, yet we continued to talk, giggle, and squirm. Not long afterward, we were promised a spanking when we got home.

When we arrived home, we ate lunch and my dad started watching Sunday afternoon football. I thought he had forgotten all about our promised discipline. At halftime, we were called, one at a time, into the bathroom—that is where Dad held his private disciplinary conversations with his children. I courageously volunteered to go first because I was the oldest and wanted to protect my siblings. As soon as the door closed, I started screaming and crying. My dad said, with amusement in his voice, "Sister, I have not even spanked you yet." Then I got the "it's going to hurt me more than it is going to hurt you" speech. I feared my dad, but I was not afraid of him. I respected him. After my promised punishment, my dad said something that has remained with me to this day: "*I have to discipline you to teach you. I told you that you would be punished and now I have to keep my word. I want you to depend upon my word just like you do my love.*"

I believe our Creator wants us to know the same thing. We may not like the discipline that comes into our lives via boot camp, as I referred to earlier, but in times of transition from the known to the unknown, we need to know that our Creator can be depended upon. In my journal, I recorded a quote someone once sent to me.

To fear the Lord is to recognize God for who He is and who He says He is. Holy, almighty, righteous, pure, all-knowing, all-powerful, all-wise, and in control of this crazy planet. When we regard our Creator correctly, we regard ourselves correctly. When we recognize who our Creator is, then we recognize our place in His plans. We then fall at His feet in humble respect and only then will He show us the way—the way chosen for us.

We need a big God. We need to understand who our Creator is and fear Him. How does this happen? For me, it is very often in creation. That is where God really shows off. It is where He communicates to me that He is all I will ever need and that He alone is big enough to carry me through all of my life's transitions.

When my circumstances seem scary and overwhelming, which I feel when change is coming, I go for a hike. When my problems threaten to engulf me or when I feel my Creator is leading me to do the impossible, I immerse myself in creation. I need to feel small. I need wide-open spaces.

During the time before our move, one of my favorite places to hike was high atop a cliff called Devil's Slide, located on Highway 1. One shoulder of the highway is the Pacific Ocean and the other is the face of a cliff. It is a treacherous, beautiful drive. Devil's Slide is a vista point with a trailhead that leads up to a higher lookout. I would climb that hill, watching the highway and the cars become smaller and smaller.

As I climbed, I became aware of the smell and sound of the ocean. That part of the Pacific coast is wild, untamed, and fierce. The waves roar and slam violently against the rock walls. I stood with my feet on the edge of the cliff, staring out into the vast ocean. In that moment, I felt like I was the only person on the planet. The thundering waves pounded at my soul. The wind whipped at a frenzied pace. I stood as still as I could and felt the power of creation and the power of my Creator. I was in awe. My world and my struggles instantly seemed inconsequential. The impossible became possible.

I have also been awed at the *bigness* of my Creator at the top of Half Dome in Yosemite National Park. I have only had the courage to make it up the infamous cables twice. It is a grueling all-day hike, topped off with a harrowing climb up a slick granite rock face holding onto cables with your hands—praying you do not slip and fall into the abyss. However, the effort is worth it. When you stand on the top edge of that enormous slab of granite, the expansive green valley below seems to disappear under the massive rock. Looking down and focusing my attention on the valley floor, I can barely make out the movement below. Cars look like Hot Wheels in a tiny toy village.

The top of Half Dome is the size of a football field. I search out a crevice where I can be alone. There it happens again—I begin to feel small. As my own stature changes, everything else in my world begins to get smaller too. As I shrink, I feel my Creator's majesty in the mountains. I feel my Creator's peace in the green pastures and His presence in the vista. I welcome it all. I do not have to have all the answers. I do not have to know the future because my Creator does.

Another secret to grace-filled transitions is knowing I am small and my Creator is big.

When transition looms, I am often uncertain of what I will need or the right path to take. But God knows. All the insurmountable obstacles my brain imagines are no match for His love for me. When I consider the force of the ocean or majesty of the mountains, the challenges in my life that seem so daunting now appear insignificant. I receive confidence that my Creator is big enough to handle anything I encounter on this planet. Fearing Him makes it all possible.

I need a big God if I am ever going to leave the known for the unknown. At this particular time in my life, it involved an unplanned move and an enormous debt.

Looking Back

Looking back is a great way to gain perspective on previous transitions in your life and prepare us for more in the future. Often when we are in the middle of change or transition, it is hard to see what purpose the event serves in moving us toward our destinies. Often, we gain fresh understanding only after the transition is complete. Trying to figure it all out while in the middle of it can prove frustrating and confusing.

However, when we begin to settle into a new comfort zone, we can review the transition, looking for the "aha" moments of how we were being moved further into our water-walking, giant-slaying, history-making destinies.

When we look back through the proverbial lens of time, we begin to realize transitions are not random acts of fate, but events orchestrated uniquely by our Creator to prepare and propel us into our unique purpose. Without them we would never go. I would have never left the Bay Area without the financial storm. That storm created the perfect situation for my inaugural water walking. Peter, our fisherman turned water walker, also encountered a storm on the night he walked on water. I wonder if he contemplated his transition many years after the fact. He was a capable fisherman quite comfortable in a boat out on the open sea. However, on his own, he knew he could not get out of that boat and walk on water. No matter how capable we may think we are, belief in ourselves alone is not sufficient to change the world. Our Creator must orchestrate transitions tailored specifically for us.

Have you reviewed yours? Now that they are over, can you see past your fear and consider if there was a divine hand moving you from the known to the unknown? Was a storm required to move you from where you were to where you were supposed to be?

Our knee-jerk reaction to difficult situations, divine or not, is to hunker down in the bottom of the boat, quaking in fear. But if we can look at transitions as divinely orchestrated methods to get us to move from where we are to where we are supposed to be, it can help us gain confidence in the process. Remembering the past helps us see how we are constantly being prepared for our future. Looking back is a secret that helps transition us to the journey ahead.

After all these secrets of transitions, you may be thinking you are ready to go. You have a divine invitation and a healthy fear of your Creator, and you are now seeing how your circumstances have been uniquely orchestrated to transition you from where you are to where you are supposed to be—but wait! The journey to your water-walking, giant-slaying, history-making destiny requires that you must leave some things behind.

Let Go!

Before you throw your leg over the side, there is something very important that must happen first. You have to let go. You have to loosen your grip on all that you think is yours, on all that you hold dear, on all that keeps you safe and comfortable.

The big secret here is that graceful transitions are impossible when you are holding tightly to something or someone.

It does not matter whom or what you are holding onto—ideas, relationships, homes, jobs, or thought patterns. Clutching anything or anyone too tightly is a certain recipe for disaster. You have to let go. If you do not, whatever "it" is may be pried from your hands—and trust me, that is not fun.

Repeat after me: "Just let go!"

A friend once asked if I had ever had my heart broken. I said no. However, the question stayed with me for a few days, tugging at my memories. It shocked me when I realized my heart had been broken twice by the same person, my eldest son. It was not intentional on his part. The only reason he had the power to break my heart was because of the death-grip I had on him. For his sake and mine, he was pried him out of my hands. Twice.

The first time it happened, I did not learn my lesson very well. I just re-gripped him and held on tighter. The second time was as painful as the first, but I finally learned a truth that startled me even more than the pain, one that ultimately allowed me to let go: my Creator loves my son more than I do.

By letting go, I learned that there was a unique plan for my son's life that was bigger and grander than anything I had ever imagined. My son's choices were his own. From then on, I got the pure pleasure of just loving him for who he is. By letting him go, he was free to become he person he was created to be. I learned that by holding onto him so tightly, I had stopped him from growing into that man.

The secret is, if you want to transition gracefully, you must *loosen your grip*, especially on those you love, for your sake and theirs.

I also had to learn this secret with regard to "things." I had to practice loosening my grip daily on the things I thought were mine. Every paycheck was an opportunity to give to others, not just meet my own needs. Giving helped loosen my grip. Every time I pulled up in my driveway, I practiced releasing my house, thankful for the privilege of its use, but reminding myself that I must be willing to give it up if I wanted to fulfill my destiny.

When I heard the still, small voice from within me whisper, "*Sell the house,*" I was able to say yes only because I had practiced releasing it daily. Of course I was sad—I'm not superhuman—but I was not devastated or distraught. Letting go of something that meant it was time for a new transition in my life.

We also had to let go of our 401(k) and the kids' college funds—all to reduce the business losses. I remember crying, "This our savings, our family's security for the future!" Then again, I felt a whisper I attributed to my Creator, saying He would be my security and my savings account, and that, as His child, I could trust in His love for me and my family.

Other times I have had to let go of a career, a position I loved as well as relationships that were important to me. It was difficult, but in time I saw that letting go was divinely orchestrated to move me further into my destiny.

Letting go of people and things loosens our grip and allows us to transition from the known to the unknown gracefully. When we give, we can expect to receive. What are you holding on tight to that may be keeping you from your world-changing destiny? Loosen your grip and see what happens. Your destiny is worth it.

Two days after our house sold, I went to church and started telling people we were moving. Over and over our friends asked, "Where?"

"I don't know," I answered. At first, I felt ridiculous uttering those words, but then I remembered the lessons I learned in boot camp and during other transitions. *I do not know* is a perfectly acceptable answer. My Creator does. That lessens my stress. I remembered that my Creator promised to lead me in the path He had chosen for me. It was not my responsibility; my family and I would be shown a path that aligned with our destiny.

During one of these conversations, a friend of mine said, "I have a rental house in Sacramento. My tenants gave their notice last night. Want to move to Sacramento?" Sacramento. I had never been to Sacramento. I did not know a soul in Sacramento.

Was this a divine invitation? I asked my husband. He answered, "Whatever." Then I asked my Creator. "Yes," was the divine answer I sensed. We immediately let go of all we held dear and headed east to Sacramento. I was confident my destiny was there, but it was not easy on any of us.

Transitions Require Perseverance

Even when we know our invitation is divine, it can still be hard. No one promised water-walking, giant-slaying, history-making destinies would be easy. If this destiny thing were easy, everyone would be doing it! Pursuing a life of purpose requires a fierce determination not to quit in the face of adversity. To transition from the known to the unknown, you are going to need some teeth-gritting, nose-to-the-grindstone, *divinely bestowed tenacity*. It is another secret to successful transitions.

However, it must be coupled with an awareness of a purpose that is greater than your immediate circumstances. I was trying to do that as we unpacked in our new rental home, but it was hard.

We tend to quit if we do not see there is a purpose—something bigger than ourselves—in the midst of our difficult circumstances, insurmountable obstacles, and painful experiences. We grow weary and lose heart when we do not understand the *why*. Earlier, I told you that others are waiting for you to have the courage to be and do all that you were created to. It matters if you are being you. It matters to someone if you quit. Your destiny is designed to meet the needs of others. Use this thought to motivate you through whatever storm you are facing.

"We are considered blessed when we persevere." James 5:11.

I laughed when I first read that. I think someone sent it to me as encouragement. However, I do not *feel* very blessed when I am in the midst of some teeth-gritting, painful persevering. I *feel* anything but blessed. However, we learned in boot camp that our feelings are not necessarily the truth. We must *choose* to believe that it matters that we persevere. It matters that we overcome, for there is a purpose—something bigger that we cannot see, and that pain and suffering will eventually lead to a blessing if we do not quit.

The fulfillment of our destinies depends upon us not quitting. I have this fear that I am going to miss what is planned for me. That is why I do not give up. It is why I have resolved not to quit. I believe there is a great harvest coming if I do not become weary doing good. When I am not seeing results or when my circumstances are not changing as fast as I think they should, this vow is my motivation. I believe it means that my efforts, my prayers, and my suffering will not be in vain. I see purpose in my efforts even when I do not immediately see the outcome I desire. The promise of my destiny tells me to work hard, not give up, and that in time I will walk on water. I must persevere. But I still hate that word. My default mode likes easy, but I know I was designed for so much more. You are, too. Take courage. Do not quit.

I chose to believe all of this as we said good-bye to our friends in the Bay Area and started a new life in our new home in Sacramento.]This took Perseverance.

I was raised by parents who both grew up on farms, so I love analogies about growing things. I learned that for crops to grow, the soil has to be prepared, the seeds planted, and the ground watered—all by the farmer. In order to ensure a good harvest, the farmer must be vigilant about protecting his garden from weeds and pests.

This is a picture of perseverance, of working for that which is unseen—another of our secrets for successful transitions.

As any farmer will tell you, there is a tremendous investment of time, energy, and money spent before the first green sprouts in a garden ever appear. The farmer participates in this backbreaking process because he is confident that his efforts will result in a harvest. He perseveres for a purpose. He works with the harvest in mind. He knows his efforts matter.

So can we.

We can have the same confidence that our work, our waiting, our sometimes-difficult transitions are all a part of the plan to transition us from the known to the unknown, the place where we will find our purpose. We must participate in the process.

Why are perseverance and participation preferred methods for transitioning into our destinies? Let's be honest; neither feels fun or divine. But which will a teenager appreciate more, a car given to him by his parents or one he buys after saving for years? Which will he take better care of and be more responsible for? The car he had to work for, of course.

We all know it is true. It is human nature. Most of us loathe the word *perseverance* because the implication is that it is going to require hard work and commitment. We like fast and easy. Perseverance is neither. Nor does it feel good or natural. But then again, neither does walking on water or transitioning into the unknown. However, it is exactly what we were created to do. Instead of fighting against it or worse, quitting, we must *choose to participate in the process.* Our Creator knows us—what we value and hold onto—and He uniquely orchestrates circumstances that require our perseverance for the privilege of participating in His divine purposes and plans for this world.

Now that makes me want to try harder, run faster, and, most importantly, it keeps me from quitting when I cannot see immediate results.

This was my perspective on the morning our moving van pulled into the driveway of our new home in Sacramento. None of us felt excitement, but I was confident we were transitioning into our destiny. This gave me the motivation to make the conscious decision to actively participate in the process. I chose to do what I could do. I slapped a smile on my face, unpacked our boxes, and made our new house a home for our family. I chose to believe in my destiny and not give up in spite of my feelings. I took control of my negative thoughts, which ultimately changed the way I felt and acted. My efforts affected others.

Little by little, our family and business grew stronger and the dream that had been laid on my heart in the Bay Area became real. It would not have happened without this difficult transition. On Christmas morning, months after the move, I woke up and sensed a silent whisper: *You did not lose your home and have to move because of financial ruin. Your financial situation was the impetus, the uniquely orchestrated circumstances I used to get you to the place where I will birth the dream I placed on your heart. You did not do anything wrong. I moved you. Here is where you will fulfill your destiny.*

Peace flooded my soul. Those words gave me courage.

Take Courage

Are you going through a difficult transition or unwanted change? I pray my story gives you encouragement. Changes are scary because they require that we leave a place we know and travel to one we do not. They leave us feeling inept and unsure. They paralyze us, making it feel impossible to advance. Those feelings are not truth. You can do this—one step at a time, one day at a time. There is a plan and purpose for your life. The blessings will come if you choose to persevere and participate in the process. Will you? Resolve right now to take every negative thought and feeling captive so you can move forward to fulfill your purpose on this planet. Take courage.

Courage is simply action in the face of fear.

It is not a feeling or a personality trait; it is an intentional choice—something you *do*, not something you *feel*. This was a revelation to me, and I learned another secret to successful, grace-filled transitions: You must take courage.

As we were settling into our new life, Michael joined me and Jake on our morning walks. As we walked and talked, a new level of intimacy was birthed in our marriage. One morning, I realized I had never told Michael the dream-filled destiny within my heart. However, the thought of doing so scared me to death. I did not want my husband to think I was crazy, or worse—*religious*. It would take an enormous amount of courage for me to tell my husband the extent of those dreams.

With courage, I concocted a plan. I took my husband out for dinner, ordered a fabulous bottle of wine, and shared the dreams I secretly carried. Nervously I began to speak, pouring out my heart and all the dreams that had been locked away for so long—an international non-profit organization, speaking engagements around the world, a book, homes called Courage Houses, and income generators that included an exclusive merchandise line and Courage Cafés. I was talking ninety miles an hour. Through it all, my husband did not say a word. I never gave him a chance. His face never once betrayed his thoughts. As I laid out my dreams, I began to *feel* foolish.

In light of our financial circumstances, these dreams made no sense. As I spoke them aloud for the first time, they sounded crazy, even to me. However, I believed them all. When I finished, I took a deep breath and poured another glass of wine, waiting for my husband to speak. When he did, I almost fell off my chair.

"The only thing stopping you is the anchor you have placed around your own neck."

I caught my breath as I grasped the fact that my husband believed in me more than I believed in myself. Revelation dawned. My fear had been self-imposed. My feelings were not truth! What if I had listened to the voices of doubt and kept silent? Without courage, I would have never heard his words or experienced the elation I felt at that moment.

I had walked through the invisible wall of fear. Confidence surged within me. My husband's belief fueled the dreams in my heart and gave me courage to take steps toward making them a reality. Yes, I was still scared. My dreams were huge and seemed impossible. I felt paralyzed by the sheer weight of them, but I declared fear would never rob me of anything ever again—especially my destiny. That night, while talking with my husband, I realized that courage simply meant moving forward one step at a time, even when I felt afraid. Courage was a choice, not a feeling. This was an eye-opening, life-changing discovery for me.

It was the same for Ordinary, a character in Bruce Wilkinson's book *The Dream Giver.*

With every step back toward the middle of Familiar, Ordinary grew more comfortable. But he quickly noticed he was also growing sad again. And he knew why; with each step he took, he was leaving his Big Dream farther behind. Then he heard the Dream Giver again.

"Why are you going back?" he asked.

Ordinary stopped. "Because I'm afraid! Leaving Familiar feels too scary and too risky."

"Yes, it does."

"But if I was supposed to do this Big Dream," Ordinary exclaimed, "then I'm sure I wouldn't feel so afraid!"

"Yes, you would," said the Dream Giver. "Every Nobody does."

Ordinary hung his head. He thought for a moment. "But you could take away the fear. Please take the fear away!" he begged. "If you don't, I can't go on!"

"Yes, you can," the Dream Giver said. "Take courage, Ordinary."

And then he was gone. Ordinary saw his choice clearly now. He could either keep his comfort or his Dream.

Which will you choose?

We all get scared and long for comfort and security. Daily we must ask for the courage to move outside our comfort zones, through the invisible wall of fear. Fear cheats us. Fear is designed to stop us from proceeding into our history-making futures. Fear entices us to settle for mediocrity. It makes us afraid to cast off the anchor we have hung around our necks.

Fear makes us believe we are less than we are. Taking courage, moving forward through your fear, is another secret to successful transitions.

Do you have the courage to be you—the you that you were created to be? Prove it. Set a goal. Speak your dream aloud. Tell someone you are going to do what scares you. Take intentional steps toward your dream, regardless of your circumstances and in spite of your fear. That is courage. Come on, get out of that boat.

I hope that by now you are encouraged to embrace the transition or change you are facing right now. I wrote this chapter hoping you would begin to see transition and change in a different light, realizing that your destiny lies outside your comfort zones in the middle of the unknown.

When a divine invitation has been issued, you will be taught many lessons as your Creator orchestrates unique circumstances to transition you from where you are to where you are meant to be. You must choose to persevere and participate in the process because something is going on that is much bigger than you. You will be required to loosen your grip on the things and people you love. Courage will be required as you walk through the invisible wall of fear that is keeping you from moving forward.

Do not Forget Your Battle Buddy

But before you head out into the unknown, there is one final secret I have found to be essential for successful grace-filled transitions to your water-walking, giant-slaying, history-making destiny. You need *intimate, authentic relationships*. Not just any relationships, but relationships with others who have left their comfort zones, given up all they held dear, and transitioned into their world-changing destinies.

During transitions from the known to the unknown, you will probably feel alone in spite of your Creator's intangible presence and still, small whisper. Often, we need the tangible company of another person who is just a few steps ahead of us, fighting for his or her destiny too. Sometimes we all need a word of encouragement or a swift kick in the butt to get us moving. Sometimes I need the encouragement of someone who has walked through his or her own invisible wall of fear and experienced a successful, grace-filled transition. I need someone to believe in me. I need my battle buddy.

We were created to be in relationship and community with others. We are designed to need and complement each other. Intimate, authentic relationships with others are a prerequisite for successful transitions. They give us the courage to move.

When I sense a divine invitation into the unknown, the only people I want to talk to, or want praying for me, are other experienced water walkers. I do not find them very often in my comfort zones. The other people who surround you in your boat of comfort are usually not water walkers either. When you are transitioning from the known to the unknown, the non–water walkers in your life will try to hang onto your leg so you cannot be and do all God has called you to do. They will call you crazy. Once you start trying to get out of your boat, you will stir some things up for them. You will rattle their cage of comfort. You will rock the boat, and most people do not like that. They like the status quo. They like you in their comfort zone.

When you begin transitioning toward your water-walking, giant-slaying, history-making destiny, you will leave people alone in their mediocrity. My advice? Do not look back. If they are hanging on your leg, shake them off and keep on going. Do not let anyone hold you back. Do not let anyone speak negativity into your life or tell you that you cannot do what your destiny calls you to do. Do not listen to them. *You get to choose who will speak into your life.*

Find some water walkers and hang out with them. You might get a little wet, but it is better than never getting out of the boat and never having the courage to be you. Ask questions about how they found the courage to get out of their boat. Find people who have persevered through difficult circumstances, courageously believing in God for their harvest. Have them pray for you. Have them speak truth to you. Read your Bible or other books of faith, and read biographies of water walkers, giant slayers, and history makers and do what they did.

Be courageous. *Do something.*

I now know our move to Sacramento was a strategic transition designed uniquely for me and my family. At the time, I had no idea how pivotal this transition would be to discovering and fulfilling my destiny. There were days when I wondered if it would ever turn out as I believed.

There was a point six months after the transition when I was very discouraged. The dreams I carried inside of me still lay dormant, hidden away with no visible means of ever happening. One night during this time, I had a dream while I slept. This dream proved "divine" to me in gaining a new perspective about my circumstances. In my dream, we were moving to a new city. My entire family was squished into a moving van, along with all of our belongings. We pulled into the driveway of the house we bought. It was small, old, and dark, located right under a freeway. The front yard was a sidewalk. I walked inside and saw there was not a window in the entire place. It was ugly and smelled of mold and mildew. The noise from the freeway was deafening. It sounded like the cars and trucks were driving right through the house. I *hated* this place. I could not believe we had bought it. I began to lug boxes into the house, feeling so alone. There was heavy darkness all around me and I kept thinking, *I am stuck here— nothing will ever change.* This was not what I had hoped for. I continued to drag in boxes from the truck. After a while, I had filled the little house with boxes, but the truck was still half-full of our stuff. The rest of our things would not fit. I was miserable.

Then I woke up.

For days, the dream haunted me and heaviness wrapped around me like a blanket. I could not shake the feelings of doom and gloom. I usually do not have dreams, much less remember them so vividly. I am not prone to visions, and I do not usually walk around with heaviness and darkness surrounding me. When I finally consulted my Creator, I sensed these words:

The dreams you carry were placed there by me and will not fit into your present circumstances, so do not even try. Do not trust what you see, trust me. I will birth what I have planted within you when the time is right.

The heaviness lifted. I was encouraged and I held onto my dreams.

Every transition I have gone through has been worth it. Each one has revealed new things about me and my destiny. Your transitions will do the same for you.

Transitions never *feel* easy and most often never *feel* good. It is dangerous to trust your feelings since they often change and are not reliable indicators of truth. I did not feel like moving to a new city. I did not feel like leaving my life in the Bay Area. I felt scared, lonely, and sad. However, time proved that my feelings were not telling me the truth about my situation. Do not despair if your dreams will not fit into your circumstances. Change is just around the corner—a transition to move you from where you are to where you are supposed to be. Embrace them.

Embrace Your Transitions

I pray that you will embrace the transitions and change in your life as divinely orchestrated circumstances leading you to your water-walking, giant-slaying, history-making destiny.

Key Chapter Concepts to Consider

- a divine invitation;
- a healthy respect for and fear of your Creator;
- a loose grip on all you hold dear;
- perseverance through difficult circumstances with confidence in the *bigger* picture;
- courage in the face of fear; and
- a few water walkers who stand beside you and believe in you.

You can count me as a battle buddy. Exciting times are coming. However, I must warn you: you are going to look a little crazy.

CHAPTER 12

The Courage to Seem Crazy

"Let us build here a church so great that those who come after us will think us mad ever to have attempted it."

Etched above a cathedral in Seville, Spain

In March 2007, I sensed it was time—time to move forward into my destiny, including producing courage conferences, writing books and building homes for those who needed them as had been whispered to my spirit. You have to understand, nothing had changed in our circumstances. We were still living in my friend's rental house, not knowing a single soul, still struggling financially, and at the same time one of my sons was being bullied at school. However, right in the middle of all that mess, I felt the whisper of my Creator, the issue of a divine invitation. And I freaked out.

I am not ready. I do not have anything to say. I have too much to say. I am scared. I have not spoken on a stage in two years. Who will listen? Everyone will think I am crazy. I do not have time. I do not have any money. Two of my kids are still at home. They need me. I do not know anyone in this town. How do I plan and market something without knowing a living, breathing soul in this town? Who live in these homes, these Courage Houses? How will I pay for it? What if no one comes? What if no one wants to read my book?

The words poured from my mouth, revealing what was in my heart—

the false belief I had claimed in the months since our move from the Bay Area. I had come to believe and own the fact that I was responsible for all the results. Oops. Paralyzing fears, clamoring doubts, and glaring inadequacies rushed forward unrestrained. I truly could not imagine how I would do what was asked of me. It all seemed so impossible. The answer was simple: *Alone, I could not.* Running outside to the wide-open spaces, hiking a mountain to feel small, and listening for the still, small voice of my Creator, I took my thoughts and feelings captive. I listened again for the divine invitation to come out on the water. However, this time I reminded myself that I was not responsible for the results. My job was to participate in the process. I had a funny feeling that the steps of faith I was about to take were going to make me look a little crazy. Thank heaven my husband believed in me.

Up until that time, I had closely guarded all the dreams I carried in my heart. My husband was the one person I had shared everything with. I pondered why. Fear. Fear of looking crazy. Fear that no one would believe me. Fear that I would not have the answers when they asked me how I was going to pull it all off so I remained silent. Now I knew my Creator wanted me to tell everyone, and I mean *everyone*, all the dreams hidden inside of me. This was my act of courage, my leap of faith.

Courage Houses, Courage Cafés, Courage Conferences, Courage Consulting, Counseling & Coaching, as well as international travel and speaking. Though I believed it all, I was not sure anyone else would. It seemed the dreams deposited within me and the ways they were going to happen would only come to fruition if I began to speak them aloud. I needed to *go out on a limb*. But what if I couldn't do it? What if people laughed? What if I was crazy and had made it all up?

What if? What if? What if?

I had a choice. I could remain silent, being more concerned for my reputation than the fulfillment of my destiny, or I could speak aloud all I believed and see if the mountains moved and the divine happened.

I chose to speak.

In that simple act of faith, the simple yet crazy and scary act of speaking, I came to believe in the fullness of my destiny. My voice was the vehicle of birth. I then wrote down everything that I believed. I called it a business plan, but it was more of a vision statement. I was taking shorthand from heaven.

The Inevitable Happened

When I got the courage to speak it all aloud to anyone who would listen, the inevitable happened—exactly what I feared. People told me I was crazy. People told me I could never do what I believed I was created to do. People read my vision statement and told me it was *too much*, that it was *too big*, and some even accused me of *trying to change the world*. I felt like they told me my baby was ugly! Some people did not even believe what I had written was divinely inspired or my destiny. Shocking, right? But guess what … I did not die of shame or embarrassment like I thought I would. I now knew *who* I was, so I kept speaking my dreams aloud, believing in them instead of my circumstances. I was not deterred or swayed by what others said. I persevered and kept moving forward.

I also learned a valuable lesson during this crazy period. My looking crazy was not about me. It was another boot camp designed by my Creator uniquely for me. The courage to be crazy was a test to see if I was trustworthy—if I could be trusted with a water-walking, giant-slaying, history-making destiny. Did my destiny mean more to me than people's opinions? Would I sacrifice my reputation and my comfort zones for all I believed? I learned that I needed to care more about my destiny than I did about myself. I needed to care more for the approval of my Creator than I did for that of other people. I learned to perform only for the audience of One—even if I did look a bit crazy. This was all a part of my boot camp. Small missions given to test my resolve to be and do all I was created to.

I believe all of heaven cheered as I ran around looking crazy, speaking truth that would lead me to fulfill my destiny.

I remember one of my first scary acts of speaking it out loud. I stood on a stage in a small church in Elk Grove, California, in front of about a hundred women. We had an amazing two days together at a Courage

Conference in which I challenged them to be all they were created to be. After it was over, I announced to them that we would meet in one week and that I would have for them a six-week workbook called the Uniqueness Assessment. That may not sound very crazy to you, but to me it was beyond crazy because I had not written a single word of that assessment. It remained unwritten except in my heart. I was scared to death when I said that aloud. The words flew out of my mouth. It was crazy! I had the title of that workbook several years prior, but I had not had the courage, nor did I believe I had the time, to sit down and write due to our transition and move to Sacramento. But on that day, on that stage in front of those women, I knew that they needed that assessment, that encouragement to be a vehicle to move them from where they were to where they were supposed to be. So I said it aloud and it was birthed in the heavens. Speaking it aloud (plus the thought of letting down those precious, courageous women) gave me the courage to sit down and write, all night long for days at a time.

I cannot adequately explain what happens in the spiritual realm when we give words to the secret dreams of our heart. The most amazing and supernatural things happen when we speak aloud the dreams and destinies we believe are deposited deep within us—crazy things happen as we see them fulfilled.

I do believe there is an intimate time with our Creator when dreams are too precious and new to share. They need to remain hidden away in our hearts until they and we have the time to grow and mature, until we believe in them and long to see them fulfilled.

When the Time is Right

But babies must be born. They cannot stay hidden forever. A restlessness sets in just as it does for an expectant mother and father. You are impatient, ready for things to happen. You are no longer satisfied with the secret of the dream, and though you are scared to death, you want to share it with the world. You are willing to risk being called crazy or being misunderstood.

I believe all of heaven smiles at this time. You finally have the courage to be you.

Undaunted, you are ready for your marching orders—for your water-walking, giant-slaying, history-making destiny. You do not care what others may say or even if all hell is trying to silence you. You are courageous—even bold—though you may look a bit crazy. Keep speaking those dreams into being. Your Creator is on your side. He is not setting you up for failure or trying to embarrass you. If He put a dream inside of you, be confident that He intends to fulfill it.

Do you feel pregnant with possibilities? Are you restless to begin? If so, then maybe your Creator is ready to start moving heaven and earth's resources to fulfill them. Write down all the seeds of destiny that have been deposited within you. Maybe, just maybe, it is time for you to speak up. Confidently begin to share your dreams with others. It does not matter whether they cheer you on or tell you that you are crazy. Your job is to speak and believe. It is impossible to remain silent when you believe you have been created on purpose for a purpose. It would be like trying to keep a baby from being born. Impossible.

Your words and your belief are powerful forces that cause heaven and earth to move.

"Shout it aloud, do not hold back. Raise your voice like a trumpet." Isaiah 58:1

These words were written thousands of years ago but are still relevant today. Can you feel their urgency? The world is waiting for you to fulfill your destiny.

Pause and listen to your own heart, your own spirit. Has your Creator deposited a dream or desire in you that you are now to begin speaking aloud? Do it seem crazy or impossible to attempt on your own? Would it feel different if you removed the burden and personal responsibility of fulfilling that dream? Would you then dare to tell people or at least email them? You can even email me.

I too have to remind myself that it is not my job to produce results. It is my Creator's. This relieves so much stress and pressure from my shoulders. My job is to speak and believe. When I get discouraged, I write down all of my dreams and all the things I am believing my Maker for. Then I speak them aloud, if only to my dog Jake.

Dare to Dream

I challenge you. Dare to dream, dare to imagine the impossible becoming possible in your life. You are called beloved. You have a place to belong. You were created on purpose for a purpose. Believe it. Shout it from the rooftops or to anyone who will listen. Risk being seen as crazy. What do you really have to lose ... except the fulfillment of your dreams?

As I stumbled along on my own journey, trying to daily find the courage to be the me I was created to be, I found another reason why birthing our dreams is so important. When you are being the you who *you* were created to be, people notice. They may think you are crazy at first, but if you do not quit, if you do not give up, then they too begin to long for more in their lives and entertain that they too may have a water-walking, giant-slaying, history-making destiny. You being you gives them the courage to believe that they were also created on purpose for a purpose. This, too, is part of your destiny.

Anything and everything you have to battle through to uncover your true identity and destiny is worth it. Do not fear crazy—it is proof you are heading in the right direction. Choose to believe only your Creator for your destiny.

Looking back, I shudder to think where I would have been if I had not chosen to believe my Creator for the truth about me, my life, and my circumstances. I admit there were days when I wavered with doubt, flirted with indecision, and cried a bucket of tears—but I never gave up. I never stopped believing. I pray with all my heart for you to do the same.

Fight for your identity and your destiny. There is so much at stake! Never apologize for being you. Do not play small so others feel better. Your Creator wants to wow you and wow the world. Daily find the courage to be who you were created to be and nothing more, and absolutely refuse to settle for anything less and then encourage everyone else that crosses your path to do the same. Go ahead; Shout it aloud, then stand back and watch.

Risk seeming crazy. It is a courageous act of faith—one that others will notice.

Key Chapter Concepts to Consider :

1. Your dreams may seem crazy to the other people in your life.

2. You must courageously speak your dreams out loud.

3. You being you will encourage other people.

4. You are not responsible for the results.

5. Your dreams are birthed as you speak.

CHAPTER 13

Clues to Your Destiny

B y now you are probably extremely restless and ready to know the details of your destiny. I know I was. I did not think I could wait a moment longer to begin doing whatever it was that I was created to. I wanted to jump in headfirst. However, the process took longer than I would have designed. Instead of a complete detailed how-to version of my world-changing destiny, I received clues much like breadcrumbs left on my path to purpose. That is what I hope to give you - clues to your world changing destiny. For me, the first one came once again from my childhood—my childhood dreams and desires.

My Story

I moved from Mississippi to the San Francisco Bay Area in 1992. I was thirty-two years old. I was completely unprepared for the differences in the two geographical areas. *Culture shock* was not a term I knew. I had never given much thought to California, or specifically the Bay Area, as those of us who live there call it. This place seemed like a faraway, foreign land. At this particular moment in my story, all I cared about was moving to that foreign land, far away from my home because my soon-to-be husband was already living and working there. I gave no thought to my destiny; I just wanted to be wherever he was. Because of our upcoming wedding day, I was giddy about leaving my home and the beautiful, hospitable place I was raised in called the South. As I packed my bags, I was not contemplating my identity or giving much thought to my destiny. I was just dreaming dreams of happily-ever-after with my handsome new husband, Michael, and my then-eleven-year-old son, Austin. I was so excited for the three of us to begin our new life together as a family.

On the much-anticipated day of our departure, I was gleefully saying my good-byes (and I do mean gleefully) at the airport. Mother, father, brothers, sisters, and in-laws were all there struggling to let us go gracefully. My mom was the last in line. She hugged me longer than she usually did. She is not much of a touchy-feely person so I was a little surprised. As I attempted to untangle myself from her embrace, she let me break away only slightly so that she could look into my eyes. I wondered if my mom had ever held my gaze for that long. Her eyes were saying something to me that she had difficulty expressing with words. She clung to me again, silently crying tears as her oldest baby was about to fly far away from the comfortable nest she was raised in. I broke her grip and gaze. I was so anxious to begin my new life. I picked up my suitcase and followed my husband and my son toward the tarmac to begin our new journey.

Before I could escape, my mom finally found words for the truth that was in her heart and in her eyes. "California will be your mission field." She stated this fact with great conviction. I turned, looking over my shoulder, wondering who in the world she was speaking to. Oh, it was me! What in the world was she talking about? (Did mention I had been a single mom for eight years and had just gotten married?) Mission field? I shook my head and ran for the airplane.

Until I began to pursue my purpose, I did not realize it, but that day, that moment, those words may have come from my mother's mouth, but they were a declaration of my destiny. Those words would lay buried in my heart for years until the perfect moment when my Creator would resurrect and remind me of their origin. My marriage was the vehicle used to transition me to a place I otherwise would have never chosen: California, the place I would pursue and fulfill my mission.

I smile now as I remember my mom's words. She was remembering something I had long forgotten—a promise I made at a very young age to travel the world to tell people in faraway places about a God who loved them. There were only two things I wanted to be when I was a little girl, a mom and a missionary. One carried no more weight in my heart than the other. Actually, those aspirations were much more specific and were extremely well thought out for a child as young as I was when I could first articulate them. I wanted to be a mom, but I was going to have a couple of sons and lots and lots of daughters. I also wanted to be a very specific kind of missionary: a foreign missionary in a place far, far away from Mississippi. This desire was so real and so compelling that I had told everyone of my plan by the time I was nine years old. I did not once worry about someone thinking I was crazy. Nope, I was confident.

To prove my commitment and belief in my dream, I walked the aisle at my church one Sunday morning, declaring to my pastor and all who were in attendance the seriousness of my intent. At nine years of age, I was certain of my destiny. Marriage, mom, and missionary. As I planned out my life in my little-girl mind, I would combine my two great desires into one by planning to marrying the man of my dreams and taking him, along with all my daughters and a few sons, to that faraway, exotic land like Africa or South America. I was going to major in home economics, and I would then teach the indigent population how to cook and care for their homes and families. That was my plan, my little-girl dream: marriage, mom, and missionary.

Fast-forward twenty years to when I stood at the airplane departure gate gazing at my mother as her declaration was drowned out by the airplane's engine. I was divorced, single mom leaving my home statefor the first time. At the ripe old age of thirty-two, I was going to marry for the second time a man I loved madly, accompanied by my eleven-year-old son, who I would gladly sacrifice anything for but this marriage. We were not headed to the mission field, and there were no daughters in sight. At that point, I had never traveled outside the United States and never even had a passport. My life had not turned out quite like I dreamed. In fact, I had not thought about my desire to be a foreign missionary in years. So at that particular moment in my history, my mother's declaration seemed ludicrous to me.

My expectancy and excitement regarding my new life in California was not in vain. I had no preconceived ideas about California one way or the other. I was delighted with my new home and the people I met.

Everyone loved my Southern accent and my Southern cooking even though they thought being from the South meant San Diego. They also thought my belief in God was cute. We made friends that felt like family and I birthed two more boys. I loved our life in the Bay Area. I did not know it at the time, but the Bay Area and the environment I found myself in was a strategic plan devised by my Creator just for me and my destiny.

Fast-forward to my forty-first year on this earth. I had begun asking the questions *who am I* and *why am I here*. I had begun my journey of purpose. My childbearing years were over, my tubes tied to ensure it. I had three biological sons I loved madly, and I was happy. My husband had a fabulous job, and I had even gotten a passport to go to Mexico for a vacation. Yet as I described earlier, I was restless to find my purpose. Memories came back, showing me the little girl I once was and the day I stopped being me, but months later more memories came and I remembered my passion to travel the world, my vow to testify to a loving Creator and the long-buried desire to have both sons and daughters. In that moment I felt the whispered words, *you will travel the world and you will have daughters*. I felt pregnant! Pregnant with possibilities, pregnant with the impossible. I did not understand the ramifications or exactly what it all meant, but I did realize my dreams were not dead. They were just buried.

Our Dreams

I learned something very important about our Creator and dreams on that day. Our little-girl or little-boy dreams that were deposited in us before time began are very often a road map to our destiny, a destiny that time does not negate or erase. No matter how much time it takes, our Creator longs to awaken and fulfill the dreams He gave us—even the ones we have forgotten from our childhood. Looking back to our childhood dreams and desires, we can find clues to our identity and destiny because they were there before life, our choices, and the choices of others intervened. It seems not to matter to our Creator how long it takes or what has transpired in our life; He remains in the business of fulfilling the dreams He gave.

By the time my dreams and desires were resurrected, I had walked out on a marriage, was divorced and now married for the second time. I did not have a passport and had never traveled to a faraway place. I never took home economics or ever testified aloud about a loving Creator. I had three sons who I adored and no longer longed for daughters, but could not wait to love the women they would one day marry. But now I remembered and a flicker of desire was ignited inside of me. I remembered loving being on a stage, and I felt my Creator say *you will speak to many*. I remembered writing poems sitting in a tree and I felt the words *you will write a book*. I did not know the how of it all. That was okay. I was perfectly content just knowing my little-girl dreams and desires were not forgotten, and that allowed me the courage to open myself up to the possibility of the impossible. I was going to travel the world, I was going to speak from a stage, I was going to write a book, and I was going to have daughters. It was my destiny and all the clues came from my childhood dreams!

What about you? What were your little-girl or little-boy dreams and desires? Do you remember what you wanted to be when you grew up? Have you become that? Are there any dreams and desires that have not come to be, that maybe you gave up on and buried prematurely? Ask your Creator to help you remember and resurrect them. Ask Him for clues from your childhood. Pay attention to the titles you wanted to have and the jobs you wanted to do; they too may be clues to your identity and destiny.

I have had many dreams and desires along the way. At one point, I wanted to be a chiropractor and then at another an interior decorator. Social worker, journalist, and psychiatrist also made the list for different reasons. Mom and missionary were the very first two and cheerleader came not long afterward. Some I became and others faded away, but if I study the titles or what I believed of them when I was a child, they did give me clues to who I was and what I was created to do. Chiropractor because I believe in natural healing; decorator because I love tranquil, beautiful spaces; social worker because I love to help people; journalist because I love to write; and psychiatrist because I am fascinated by human behavior. Mom because I am a nurturer. Missionary because I had experienced the love of my Maker.

Cheerleader because I am an encourager. I may have not had the job titles, but in those choices I was discovering who I was and what I was created to do. On this journey, I realized the little-girl dreams and desires of my heart were different from job titles. They were put there by my Creator to serve as a road map to my destiny. But after many years of disappointment and bad choices, I had buried them so deep that I never believed they could be fulfilled.

When I first started this journey of uncovering my identity and discovering my destiny, I did not even remember my childhood dreams. If I had, I would have probably shrugged them off as mere childhood fantasies. I had no idea I was settling for less than what was planned for me.

Friends, be encouraged! Let me be the one to speak this truth to your mind, your heart, your soul, and to your spirit. Your Creator has not forgotten your childhood dreams and the desires of your heart. If He placed them there, He intends to fulfill them. Like me, you may have to let go of your preconceived ideas of how and let your Creator orchestrate the fulfillment of them all. You will not be disappointed. I am praying right now that you have the courage to consult your Creator and ask Him to bring to memory any dreams He placed inside of you before time began that He intends to fulfill. Listen to your spirit and the still, small voice inside. Listen for clues from the past; they may just help you change the world.

Key Chapter Concepts to Consider :

1. Your childhood dreams are a roadmap to your destiny.

2. Ponder the titles of who you wanted to be when you grew up.

3. Consult your creator for the memories.

4. Your creator deposits dreams inside of you He intends to fulfil.

5. Your dreams are not dead they may just be buried.

CHAPTER 14

Your Passions

I wish I could tell you that after my long-buried dreams for world travel, speaking on stages, writing books, and having daughters was resurrected, the restlessness I described earlier ended. It did not. Not only did it continue, but it increased. I was ready for some action. I needed to be doing something, though not sure of what or how.

At that time, my church was advertising a class that proclaimed if I faithfully attended, I would discover my spiritual gifts. Though I had no idea what in the world a spiritual gift was, ,I felt compelled to enroll. The idea of discovering any type of gift was exciting to me since I believed I was not born with any natural talents and there was nothing gifted about me, unless you counted talking a lot.

Finding Passion

On the very first night of class, I almost quit. The first small group question after the video finished playing was posed: "What are you passionate about?" I tried to remain calm. I stared at the blank piece of paper. I felt like I needed to breathe into a paper bag. The instructions were to write down your reflections on that question, and then you would be asked to share your thoughts with the group. That caused a panic attack since I had not yet overcome my fear of public speaking. Sitting in a chair surrounded by fifteen other people qualified as such. I did not want to share. I did not have anything to share.

I had just told my husband the week before how I envied his passion for golf. He would go out in the cold and pouring-down rain just to hit a bucket of balls! Nothing could get me out in the cold and rain.

Nothing. My passion? The question loomed. I did not have an answer.

My anxiety mounted as the group began putting their pens down. Each person's paper was full of their passions. My paper was blank and wet from my sweaty palms. I was dreading my turn. I had no idea what I would say. For some reason, it felt hideously wrong to say I did not have a passion. The process began and around the table we went. I prayed I would be last. I started getting an icky feeling in the pit of my stomach, the same one I had when I was called to the principal's office as a little girl. Impending embarrassment and humiliation. Finally, my name was called. "Jenny? What are you passionate about?" I felt like I was going to faint.

The facilitator must have recognized my anguish because she embellished the question a bit more by saying, "What could you sit and do for hours and hours?" First of all, this was so the wrong question for me—I do not sit for hours and hours and "do" anything! Sitting still is not one of my talents or abilities. My mind was filled with random thoughts like these as I stalled for time.

Then a new phenomenon occurred. I was struck mute. Rarely have I been rendered speechless. I could not say a word, but tears welled up in my eyes threatening to spill over onto my already perspiration-soaked blank piece of paper. I felt like I was in back in grade school. Everyone was staring at me. Three seconds of silence can be agonizing.

Then suddenly from somewhere deep inside of me, without any rehearsed thought, my mouth opened and out burst the cry of my heart. "I am passionate about everything. I have a passionate opinion about everything and nothing. I am so passionate I wear myself out on a daily basis."

The facilitator smiled a knowing smile. I wondered if she knew something I did not. As the words left my mouth and the sound traveled up to my ears, I knew in my spirit it was truth. My problem was not a lack of passion. It was an overwhelming abundance of it. It was what I had been criticized for most all my life.

I was shocked myself. How can you be passionate about everything but no one thing? I say yes to any and everything anyone asks me to do. My hand shoots up to volunteer of its own accord. In my spirit, I am screaming *pick me*—for anything. I did not know if I was truly passionate about everything or if I just liked be included.

I left the class feeling more restless and ordinary than ever. What was I to do with this new self-awareness? The facilitator had given us a homework assignment. We were to ask someone we trusted for help in defining, or, in my case, narrowing down our passions. Who would I ask? With this question the possibility of embarrassment or humiliation was reaching an all-time high. I almost quit my journey of purpose right then and there. I was holding on tight to my identity.

I am so glad I did not quit, because my answer was close by. I found the one I was longing for in the least likely place—my bed. With the least likely person—my husband. When I returned home from my class that evening, my husband was in bed watching television. I burst into the room and interrupted his favorite program on TV, golf! If the man cannot play golf, he watches it. Bursting into tears, I flung myself on his chest explaining my lack of a specific passion.

"Passionate about everything isn't an answer!" I blubbered. He was surprisingly patient with me since self-awareness is so not his thing. I told him I had to have someone help me narrowly define my passions, someone who knew me and loved me. Though he qualified as that person, I never once entertained the notion that he might volunteer his services. Calm and confident man that he is, he took the now-soggy homework paper I was clutching in my hand, skimmed over the hundreds of questions, threw it on the floor, and with great wisdom said, "I know what you are passionate about."

Time stood still. Hope welled up inside of me. Could it be this easy? The man who loves and knows me better than anyone in the entire world—could he really have my answer? My husband delivered his answer with no fanfare: "Your buddies." Sounded like golf buddies. He went on, "Your friends. They are always calling you, asking for your advice, encouragement, asking for your help with children, husbands, marriage, jobs, arguments. You are the 'Dear Abby' of our neighborhood." He lovingly concluded, "You are passionate about all women, as well as friends, family, neighbors, and complete strangers!

And you are equally passionate about your children."

Be still, my heart. He was right.

I did have a passion, and my husband had uncovered it for me. Somewhere along the path of my life, my Creator had given me a love and passion for encouraging others, at that time in my life it was for the women I loved and shared my life with. Paradoxically, I had spent most of my life hanging out with guys. My best friends have always been guys. I really did not like girls. I wanted them to be more like men—less drama, less talking, more doing.

This profound discovery of my passion, coupled with my resurrected dream to have daughters, led me to action. With my knees knocking and all the courage I could muster, I opened my home weekly to a small group of women to equip and encourage in their passions. I thought I had died and gone to heaven. I was doing something! My restlessness subsided. This group of women became the first Righteous Girlfriend Group (RGG). I was passionate about having them in my home every week. We shared our hearts, our lives, and our journeys to God. These women ultimately became my spiritual daughters. This was my first taste of my destiny—of being and doing all I was created to be and do. It was highly addictive.

Defining my passion was most difficult for me, so I hope I am making your journey of purpose easier. Passion was so nebulous. I could recognize it in others but not in myself. I did a little research on the word to help clarify exactly what a *passion* is. Webster calls it "any powerful or compelling emotion or feeling, such as love or hate." Ah, simplicity.

Just ask yourself, *what do I love, hate, or totally get emotional about?*

My thought for you as we end this chapter is that you will begin to feel a restlessness in your spirit to "do something." I pray that God will reveal to you the specific passion He deposited in you long before time began. I pray that you will have a new divine awareness of the people and situations that move you to compassion. I pray that compassion will lead you straight to action in spite of your fears and circumstances. I pray you will consult your Creator daily to be reminded of who you are and the inheritance you hold.

Your Passions

You were created on purpose for a purpose and your passions hold a clue!

Key Chapter Concepts to Consider :

1. Your passions are clues deposited by your Creator to lead you to your unique identity.

2. Others can help you identify your passions.

3. Keep doing what you love to do.

4. Pay attention to what you love, hate or get highly emotional about.

5. Let your compassion let you to action.

CHAPTER 15

Generations Before

I am so excited you have come this far on your journey of purpose. How I long to look deep into your eyes and tell you that your life matters. I long for you to know that you are created on purpose for a purpose. You, your life, and your destiny is to be a history maker, life changer, water walker, and giant slayer. Whether you realize it or not, whether you are intentional about it or not, you are impacting lives and situations daily. Good and bad, positive and negative.

Does that stop you in your tracks? It does for me. It actually boggles my mind when I take the time to ponder and contemplate the hugeness of that concept. My little life, my decisions, and my choices are greatly affecting the people around me. I can wrap my brain around believing I may have some impact on my immediate family or friends—but complete strangers or people who have not even been born yet? I did not give much thought to this until recently, when I realized how the destinies of the people who had gone before me have shaped and contributed to my own life and destiny.

I got "the call" at 6:00 a.m. on March 13, 2005. I had been waiting on this call ever since the day I moved to California. When you leave home, away from all those you call family and friends, you *know* that one day you will get "the call" that comes in the middle of the night and drives you to your knees. The one that tells you someone you have loved is gone, that his or her life has come to an end. Knowing it and expecting it does not lessen the pain when you answer it. It does not even lessen when the end is welcomed because suffering has ceased. My Mimi was gone.

I told you her name was Elizabeth and she was adopted from an orphanage. On that spring day in 2005, her spirit left her worn-out body, although her mind had been gone for a while. She was ninety-two years old. As her obituary chronicled, she was survived by two daughters, seven grandchildren, twelve great-grandchildren, and one great-great-grandchild. Funny how they sum up a life in the newspaper that way—survived by, gone before her, born, lived, died. It struck me as funny when I first read it; then I was sad because they were talking about my grandmother. My Mimi's life was so much more than a paragraph in the back of a newspaper. Her life and her choices had impacted so many people, including mine. I was determined that she was going to have a grander send off than that. Much to my surprise, because I had learned the lesson in the previous chapter, my passion led me straight to action. I was going to give her eulogy. It did not matter that I had never done a eulogy before. I just knew in my heart that it was what I had to do.

My Mimi

Before her death, I had a plan to visit my Mimi when I made my annual pilgrimage home to Mississippi. I wanted her to have a clear mind, just for a moment, so I could look into her eyes, hold her hand, and tell her how much her life, her choices, her decisions, and her obedience had impacted my life. I wanted her to know how her love for God had affected my identity and now my destiny. I wanted to thank her. I wanted to tell her that all the hardships she endured, all the rejection and pain, all the battles she fought were not in vain—they were for me, for us, and for the generations that followed her. I am quite sure she never contemplated her choices in light of how they would affect those that would come after her. However, they did and I wanted her to know that. Sadly, she left this world before I ever had the opportunity to tell her all the things stored in my heart. Instead, I gave her eulogy. I could not leave that task to the young pastor who had only known her as an old woman who had lost her mind. When he met her, she had not been my Mimi in a long time and instead was a scared little girl trapped in an old woman's body. She spent a lot of time remembering the past.

I am laughing and crying as I remember her. Even without her mind, she was a force until the day she died. My mom and aunt went to choose her casket before she died at the prompting of the doctor since she did not have much time left. However, he did not know my Mimi. No one told her what to do or when to do it—especially when to exit this world. After selecting her casket and planning her funeral, she lingered for another seven days. She was a fighter and a giant slayer until the very end. Five feet tall, 110 pounds soaking wet, and full of spit and vinegar was a common description of my Mimi. Still, she was scared to death to fly in an airplane—she never did—and to the day she died she hated being left alone or in the dark.

She was such a contradiction. My aunt told me that once, as a young girl, my Mimi ditched school, put on her roller skates, and hooked a rope to a car so she could skate around town. Fearless one moment and a frightened little girl the next. She was little but strong. Humble yet willful. She was not going anywhere until she was good and ready. I told everyone at the funeral that she probably lingered on this earth, waiting for someone in heaven to go get my Daddy-Jay (her husband) off the lawn mower somewhere in the back forty of heaven so he would be waiting to welcome her as she made her entrance into heaven. My Daddy-Jay. He had been gone for almost twenty-three years, and my Mimi missed him every one of those days. The two of them could make you believe in true love, fairy tales, and soul mates. I have the original love poems my Mimi wrote to her man. Their love for each other impacted all the lives they touched.

The Eulogy

Funny, the first people to hear her eulogy were a group of little kids. The day I received that phone call was a Sunday morning, and I was scheduled to teach the children's class at church. The story I was to teach was about David and Goliath. The focus word for the kids was *courage*. I was an emotional mess. Everything that morning reminded me of my Mimi—especially this particular story and word. As I stood before the kids, I began to tell the story of David facing the giant. I did not have to embellish the story to hold their attention. Kids just love hearing how a shepherd boy defeated a nine-foot giant armed only with a little slingshot, some common river rocks, and an enormous belief in his God.

As I finished telling the story, I promised these children that God would never ask them to fight a nine-foot giant with a slingshot. I did promise them, however, that at some time in their life—and probably more than once—He would ask them to do something that was very difficult, very scary, and could only be accomplished with an enormous belief in their Creator and all the courage they could muster. Every adult in the room nodded their agreement.

Even my little grandmother, my Mimi, had to fight a giant, was not a nine-foot-tall Philistine. It was prejudice and racism in the Deep South during the early 1940s and 1950s before there was a civil rights movement. My Mimi impacted her world in a mighty way, including complete strangers and unborn children. She crossed the proverbial tracks. She went to a side of town she was told not to go to. She loved people who were a different color than she was. She feed people and brought people into her home that was a different race than she was. She believed it was wrong to judge people by their skin color. She shared her heart, her home and her faith with any and everyone. She stood up for injustice and rescued the least of these. For her courageous efforts she received death threats and was thrown out of her own church. She did not care. LIke David, she ran towards a fight with giants armed only with truth. She had the courage to be who she was created to be and she apologized to no one for it. Because of that, lives many lives were impacted. At my grandfather's funeral years ago, an old gentleman shuffled into the funeral parlor to stand in front of me. I will never forget his words: "If it wasn't for Miss Liz and Mr. J.D., I would have never known the Lord Jesus as my Savior—'cause they had come to teach the children."

What a eulogy, what a testimony … what a legacy.

By the time I was born, my Mimi's giant-slaying days were over. I only knew her as my grandmother. My great-grandmother Eleanor rescued my Mimi from an orphanage, from an identity that said she was unwanted and had no value, to a destiny that literally changed the lives of individuals in her world because she chose to fight an injustice that many others chose to ignore. I have received blessings in my life that are a direct correlation to my Mimi's love of others and her Creator and the actions of her compassion. The ceiling of her life became the floor on which I stand gazing into my destiny. Oh, how I pray my children and grandchildren can say the same of me!

It completely boggles my mind how looking back through the lens of time can bring such clarity to my destiny. I shake my head in wonder and cry with the realization that my destiny started with a woman born in the late 1800s. A woman named Eleanor Glass, who I called Granny but is of no blood relation to me. A woman whose wedding band I now claim as my own, who fought to rescue one child from an orphanage, bestowing the identity of daughter and the name Elizabeth upon her. And who, because of that identity, went on to rescue and set free individuals of another color whom her peers said were unworthy, invaluable, and throwaways at that time. A woman who I called Mimi, whose ring I also wear as my own, changed her own world. The rescued often become rescuers. These two ordinary women and their courageous choices have radically influenced my life and my destiny long after their deaths.

Little did I know that I would one day have daughters who I did not birth, who would bear the names of these two women. Little did I know that I too would fight injustices too big for me and rescue children who would need a home, children of all different races and nationalities.

Friends, clues to our own destinies are in our family histories. There is deposited within us a desire to matter—it is part of our identity and destiny. That desire is for us to be water walkers, giant slayers, and history makers. Often there are clues in our past to the exact nature of that destiny. Are there doctors, lawyers, pastors, firemen, police chiefs, moms, or teachers in your past? Is there a tendency for people in your family to be risk takers or facilitators of other people's dreams? Ask family members who are still around if they can help you connect any dots. Talk with the oldest family members and ask them to tell you the family stories. Write them all down. Celebrate those who have gone before you and mine their lives for the treasures that can make you rich.

Do not be discouraged if you do not have access to the people or stories before you. Consult your creator—He has all your answers. If you do not have a family tree that looks like mine, you may be the first water walker, giant slayer, and history maker in your family. Your children and grandchildren will thank you.

We are on this planet to change the world, one individual at a time. Just do it! It will take courage—action in the face of our fear. For such a time as this you were born. You being you matters. It matters to this generation and to the one to come. My desire for you as you end this chapter is that you will begin to consider your legacy. How high will the ceiling you leave for the next generation be? Ignore the *what ifs* and the *how will I ever* taunts of the giant. You will be provided with all the slingshots and rocks you will ever need. Let your passion propel you into action.

Let your life be the breadcrumbs that others will follow to their unique destinies!

Key Chapter Concepts to Consider :

1. Your decisions and choices are affecting the world and generations to come.

2. Your ceiling will be your children's floor.

3. Pay attention to the stories from your family's past, there are clues and connections to your destiny.

4. Courageously run towards battles armed with truth.

5. Consider the legacy you are leaving.

CHAPTER 16

Your Unfounded Fears

I hate that I have lived most of my life afraid. Afraid of what others would think, afraid of losing my job, afraid of losing my home, afraid of losing my kids, afraid of losing my breasts, afraid of losing my husband, afraid of being embarrassed, afraid of speaking, afraid of writing, afraid of being used, afraid of going bankrupt, afraid of failing. Afraid of everything. Afraid about nothing.

I once heard that human beings are the only species that can scare itself. That's me.

Afraid, afraid, afraid.

That is why for so long I hated the word *courage*. It implied you were going to have to do something you were afraid of. I had avoided that most of my life. I believed courage was a personality trait. Either you had it or you did not. And I did not have it nor did I want it.

The further I have walked on this journey of purpose, the more I have come to love the word, for I learned it simply meant action. Action I love; it is fear I try to avoid.

Former First Lady Eleanor Roosevelt disagrees with me. She suggested you should, "Do one thing every day that scares you." My mind screams, *Why?* However, even as I ask the question, I know the answer. Doing something that scares me, something I fear, requires me to choose courage; it requires action on my part. Fear paralyzes me, but courage moves me through its invisible wall. When I break through that wall, a sense of accomplishment and confidence embraces me. After a while you become accustomed to doing things scared. With experience, you soon realize your fears, like your feelings, are not true indicators of truth. With enough practice, you will find that you do not even require courage anymore because at some point in time when you were not even aware, you have become bold. That is when you become dangerous—when you are a full-fledged member of the water-walking, giant-slaying, history-making club.

Facing Your Fears

I have found that fears can even be helpful in identifying your unique world-changing destiny. The very thing that at one time scared me the most was exactly what I was created to do. My dog, Jake, taught me that lesson.

As I mentioned before, Jake is a Labrador retriever. Labs were created on purpose for a purpose—swimming and hunting. They love to get wet and they love to fetch. They are literally made for it. Labs have a thick tail, called an otter tail, that was designed to propel them through the water at great speed to fetch the ducks their owners shot out of the sky. Their hair is much like a duck's feathers; it repels water. Getting a Lab soaking wet is a difficult feat. All Labs love water—except Jake. He did not swim or fetch. He was scared to death of the very thing he was created for.

It all started when we gave him a bath as a puppy. Bathing a dog is an unnatural act, but because Jake was being groomed to be a housedog and not a hunter, he needed to smell good if he was to be granted access to our home. On this particular day, Michael, my husband, and my two young sons, Michael-Dean and Ben, were lathering up Jake with rosemary-scented dog soap. Ben was holding Jake while my husband held the water hose. Michael-Dean's job was to turn the water on and off when his dad yelled, "Turn it on!" and "Turn it off!" The directive was shouted and Michael-Dean turned on the water. When he did, the force of the water whipped the hose out of my husband's soapy hands, hit Jake in the head and sprayed water all over his poor face. In the process, Ben got soaked, too. So he screamed, causing Jake to run out of the backyard with the entire family in pursuit. When we finally caught him, he was hiding in the neighbor's hedge. We dragged him out by his front legs. The emotional trauma that poor dog endured was severe and long lasting. Thank heaven my husband and boys were unscathed. Jake never recovered. From that day forward, Jake refused to go near *any* body of water. He would cross to the other side of the street if he saw a puddle or a sprinkler. Swimming? No way. He shook like a leaf if near any type of water.

We tried everything, even throwing him in. (In hindsight, I do not advise this course of action; it only made things worse.) Jake had become afraid of the very thing in which he was created to thrive in. Now do not feel too sorry for Jake. Though he was not being and doing all he was created to, he lived a very good, comfortable life. Though he did not swim, he loved riding in the car and was allowed to go most places we went. He loved tennis balls but never got the whole fetch thing. He was terribly afraid of rain, so we let him inside the garage because his big otter tail knocked over everything in the house. Gradually we let him come inside only if he could courageously endure a quick, fragrant bath, complete with a blow dry. (He hated blow dryers as much as water.) He liked barking at the dogs on the television. We did not let him on the couch but got him his own feather bed—which he chewed to pieces if left alone. He seemed happy with his domestication. When he was outside for any length of time, he managed to escape because he did not like to be alone. I think I rescued him seven times from the pound or from one of the neighbors who would graciously take him inside. He was always glad to see me but seemed content to stay where he was as long as other people were around. He liked people better than other dogs, thus he was never enthusiastic about doggy parks s. However, he loved our walks on the levee, yet he always remained for from the water. That is, until one day when he was about eight years old—about sixty-two in dog years.

We were on our regular daily purpose walk. I had taken Jake to our church, which backs up to the San Francisco Bay, so he could sniff and be off the leash. That day, I was not attuned to Jake's wanderings as I was contemplating my own identity and destiny. Suddenly, I saw a quick movement out of the corner of my eye. To my utter amazement, Jake was running. I mean really *running*—like a dog—straight in the direction of a large body of water that had two ducks sitting on it. It is difficult to explain what happened in those few minutes, but I can only describe it as that which Jake was created for became more powerful than his fear. I saw him gracefully fly through the air and belly flop on the water. It was a thing of pure beauty. Then he started swimming toward the ducks. They started to fly and he chased them. I do not know who was shocked more: Jake, me, or the ducks! I watched in stunned silence. (This was pre-cell phone camera days.) Jake was swimming.

On this particular day, Jake took courage. He did it scared.

Jake finished his swim and ran to my side. I swear he was smiling and that big ole fat tail was wagging at a crazy speed. Soaking wet, he shook his entire body, spraying me with water. I sank to the grass and hugged my wet dog. Laughing all alone on the wet grass, I contemplated the divine gift I had just received. It was the gift of watching my dog overcome fear and do the very thing he was created to do—the very thing that his fear had stolen. It was as if time stood still.

A tear slipped down my cheek as I hugged my very courageous dog, and I sensed these words:

You are no different from Jake. You too have become domesticated. Your fears are unfounded. The very thing you are afraid to do is the very thing I have created you for.

Now I wept. I knew it was true.

Afraid to Be YOU?

My fears seemed pitiful and small. I feared regret, failure, criticism, and laughter. I realized I only did the things I felt comfortable with and was good at. I was afraid to try anything new because my old enemy—embarrassment—just might come for a visit. I was a forty-something-year-old woman and the bottom line was that I was afraid to be me. I remembered that bold, passionate little girl and knew that fear was keeping me from fulfilling my destiny. I vowed to walk through my invisible walls of fear so that I could be and do all I was created for.

Jake was my inspiration. However, Jake had a natural instinct kick in when he saw the water and ducks; you and I must daily make the intentional choice of courage, of taking action in spite of our fear.

I began to do things that scared me—things that deep inside I longed to do and things that I had done as a child. I volunteered to lead a small group. I publically shared my testimony. I trained for a sixteen-mile hike to the top of a mountain. I led a group of women to the top of Half Dome in Yosemite National Park. I led a ministry. I spoke on a stage. I taught a class. I organized conferences. I shared my faith. I spoke up. I started a non-profit organization. I began to write a book.

I practiced being me. And I did it scared.

Cassandra's Example

Jake was my inspiration, and so was a young teenager named Cassandra.

A beautiful sixteen-year-old young woman, Cassandra attended one of our very first Courage Conferences and Uniqueness Assessment Workshops. During the second small group session, I asked if anyone had a courageous story to share. Cassandra raised her hand. She said that during the first week of the Uniqueness Assessment, she was doing her homework and she was inspired to write a song.. She wrote down the words and melody she heard that night. I was so excited when Cassandra shared this that I immediately asked if she would sing it. She quickly said, "No!" We all laughed and I offered the microphone to someone else.

The next week I arrived early to the group. I was up front as the women were entering. I saw Cassandra's beautiful curly red hair immediately—and she was carrying her guitar. I ran up to her and asked, "Are you going to perform your song?" She shyly smiled and said yes. I could not wait to tell everyone. My heart was pounding. I knew her Creator was delighted because she was about to walk through an invisible wall of fear and we, her righteous girlfriends who were much older, were getting a front-row seat at this incredible display. I was so nervous for her.

Cassandra took the microphone and told us her little-girl story. When she was six years old, she was to perform at her first piano recital. As she took her seat before the massive instrument looked out into the sea of faces, she froze. She could not remember her song. She walked away from the piano. Her piano teacher sent her back out to overcome her fear and try again. Still she froze. We all held our breaths as we remembered similar fears. At six, she walked off the stage and away from her destiny. She told us that she had not stood in front of an audience, on a stage, alone since that day. What courage she displayed. We all held our breaths as she put her guitar in place. Tears were already flowing down my cheeks. Her courage and her fear were both palpable. I whispered a prayer as she began to sing the song she had written, titled "Lord, Move My Feet."

Not a soul dared to take a breath. Cassandra and, I believe, all the angels in heaven sang together. When she finished, I did not detect a dry eye in the room. She smiled the same smile Jake did. The entire room got to their feet, clapping and cheering, celebrating the fact that it did not take Cassandra thirty years to courageously face her fears as it had for most of us. Another incredible gift. Another timeless moment when I had the opportunity to watch a courageous water walker stepped out of her boat onto the water. At that moment I prayed for my children. I prayed they would learn this lesson long before I had. I had wasted so much time.

Cassandra's mom approached her at the end of the evening and asked, "What if you had left your guitar in the car?" What I think she really meant was, "What if your fear had won? What if you had chose to stay in your boat?"

Four years later, Cassandra leads worship at her college group and at many other venues around her hometown. She has continued to write songs and perform on stages—fearless.

Friends, it is time. It is time for you to face your fears, get out of the boat of the known, and courageously walk into the unknown; it is where you will discover your world-changing destiny.

In my own journey of purpose, I have come to believe there are only a few things we should fear.

- Fear that you will settle for less than you were created for.

- Fear that you will give up and quit too soon.

- Fear that you will never attempt anything great.

- Fear that no one will ever notice you were here.

Let those fears propel you into your destiny. Take one step, any step, for it is far better to dare mighty things and experience defeat than to sit on the sidelines of life never attempting anything. It seems President and Mrs. Roosevelt agree, and both knew a thing or two about doing things that scare you.

"It is not the critic who counts; not the man who points out how the strong man stumbled or where the doer of deeds could have done them better. The credit belongs to the man who is actually in the arena; whose face is marred by dust and sweat and blood; who strives valiantly; who errs and comes short again and again, because there is no effort without error and shortcoming; who does actually try to do the deed; who knows the great enthusiasm, the great devotions and spends himself on a worthy cause; who, at the worst, if he fails at least fails while daring greatly. Far better it is to dare mighty things, to win glorious triumphs even though checkered by failure, than to rank with those poor spirits who neither enjoy nor suffer much because they live in the gray twilight that knows neither victory nor defeat."

–Theodore Roosevelt, Eleanor's husband.

Key Chapter Concepts to Consider :

1. Do one thing every day that scares you.

2. What you fear may be exactly what you were created to do.

3. Do it scared.

4. Fear paralyzes you, courage propels you.

5. Courage simply means action in the face of fear.

CHAPTER 17

I Get to Be Me!

On my forty-third birthday, I was given a card with a wish, penned by Maya Angelou, that is to this day tucked inside my Bible. I read it often.

"Today I wish for you one perfect moment when you are utterly yourself, when you are convinced you are God's own child ... when you realize that everything is within your grasp."

Today, as I write these words, I am fifty-three, and I am still enamored with these words. A moment, a perfect moment, when you are utterly yourself. I love the sound of that. I just get to be me. Sounds so simple—so freeing—but for some reason so difficult for so many of us. In the midst of seeking clues for our unique destiny, we must take time to just be the me we were created to be. We must learn to love and enjoy ourselves because we cannot love another until we love ourselves.

This is what our focus will be in this chapter—those moments when you catch a glimpse of your true self, clues to who you are and what you are supposed to be doing. The moments when you feel free. When everything is effortless. When you find your sweet spot. I was reminded of Maya's words during an encounter with a three-year-old.

A Divine Landing

Her name was Kayla. She literally plopped in my lap, completely startling me. "An angel" was my first thought. "Delightful" was my second. In that moment, I would have told you that her arrival was unplanned, maybe even random if I believed in such things. However, I would have been wrong. Time would reveal that this landing was intentional and full of purpose. This delightful, pint-sized angel would not be simply a gift for the moment, but a tender reminder of someone I lost a long time ago.

I was alone and operating in full mommy mode prior to this divine lap landing. My middle son, Michael-Dean, had band practice at our church. His first public guitar performance was scheduled for the next evening, and I had the mom task of carpooling. I comforted myself with the thought of two uninterrupted hours of inspired reading to pass the time while I waited. I had just claimed my seat on the floor with a few other carpool-weary moms and was about to get lost in my book when a swirling blond vision caught my eye. Without warning, but to my utter delight, the lovely child plopped into my lap.

My senses were overwhelmed as her strawberry-scented hair covered my face and obscured my view. I was literally wrapped in angel hair. Her tiny hand caressed my face, and she laughed as she freed her hair from mine. What came into view was clearly a beautiful angel masquerading as a three-year-old only inches from my face. Without hesitation or a proper introduction, she threw her arms around my neck and stared intently into my eyes. With stillness uncommon to children her age, she held my gaze, hypnotizing me. Though neither of us spoke, we communicated perfectly in the silence. An eternity later, she broke the spell when she asked, "Will you be my friend?" Though it was the most ordinary of questions, the words were spoken with such confidence, eloquence, and sophistication I felt I was being chosen for a great honor. My reply of "Yes" delighted her so much that she hugged me as if she had known me her entire life. Captivated, I fell completely and madly in love. I spent the rest of the evening willingly engrossed in this child-angel and her world. Joy bubbled up from my soul and tangibly displayed itself as tears in my eyes. I giggled, which is much different than laughing out loud. For I knew without a doubt that I had just been ambushed from the ordinary and thrown headfirst into the extraordinary.

In retelling the story, I am still amazed how this little pint-sized girl plopped so confidently into my lap. It still astonishes me that she did so without any apparent fear of rejection. I guess being so young, she had not yet felt the sting of that particular emotion, and I never wanted her to. So I wrapped my arms tightly around her, burying my nose deep in her hair while she talked non-stop. As she shared her angel secrets, I noticed a very serious little boy hovering nearby. I was about to speak to him when Kayla whispered in my ear, as three-year-old little girls do, that he was her big brother. By the look on his face, it was obvious he was extremely wary of my close encounter with his little sister. Suddenly, with great drama, he cupped his hands around his mouth and loudly proclaimed, "Stranger! Stranger!" to anyone who would listen—especially me. His body language actually screamed "Danger! Danger!" But my little angel ignored her brother's warning, possessively wrapping her arms tighter around my neck. Her love for me was not cautious but extremely extravagant. I felt bathed in it, even if her big brother was not amused.

The room we were in was large and had been cleared of all chairs for my son's concert the next evening. There were not many people in the room, but there were more on the stage, which was covered with instruments, amplifiers, and nervous adolescents eager, yet scared to death, to perform in their first concert. No one paid any attention to Kayla and me—except her brothers. Another brother had shown up by this time. This one, however, was not fazed at all by my love affair with his little sister. He was content to sit beside us quietly reading a book. The concerned oldest brother continued to hover nearby just in case Kayla needed to be rescued. We all listened to the band play. The music was exceptionally beautiful. This place and time seemed enchanted.

After a while, in spite of our mutual love, my little angel got antsy and needed to move her body through space. As quickly as she entered my lap, she left it. But before I could feel the ache of missing her, she reappeared in front of me. This time not to sit with me, but to perform for me. I was honored and thrilled. My little angel turned into a dancer and began spinning in circles, round and round and round. She never once got dizzy, a feat she was quite proud of and one I remembered accomplishing myself long, long ago. She danced uninhibited to the young band's music, confident they played only for her. When they paused, she ran as fast as she could across the room, flying, so she claimed, with arms outstretched, jumping in the air like a ballerina. I clapped and cheered loudly. I never once took my eyes off her. She kept looking at me, making sure I was looking at her. I was her audience of one and my undivided attention mattered greatly to her. My delight in her grew as she performed with an abandon common only to three-year-olds. She danced with all her heart, and suddenly I had the desire to do the same. But like the mature adult I was, I suppressed the urge and remained anchored to the floor.

Several times during my angel's performance, I wondered where her parents were. I was reluctant to break the spell of this magical dance, so I did not allow my thoughts to become words. Finally, my own mom mode proved stronger than the moment and I asked, "Where are your mommy and daddy?" She turned, pointing proudly toward the stage, to a man doing a sound check at the microphone. With the mystery solved of where her parents were, my angel continued her performance. After a while, the now-identified daddy of my angel eventually wandered over to introduce himself. Or maybe he thought Kayla and I were too intimate for strangers and wanted to make sure my intentions were honorable. If that was the case, I truly wanted to ease his fears. So before he spoke, I blurted out that I had fallen madly in love with his daughter. It is a wonder he did not think I was crazy. However, he only smiled and nodded as if this was a most common phenomenon with his daughter. Was I not the first to be so captivated and chosen? I rejected the thought.

We chatted some more, and I guess I passed the stranger safety test because my friend's daddy returned to the stage, confidently leaving Kayla and I to walk hand in hand to the ladies' room. Her trust in me had no boundaries. Like good girlfriends do in the bathroom, we shared some lip gloss and a hairbrush after we washed up. As we walked back to the auditorium, my angel-turned-dancer decided that walking was way too boring. She suggested we skip. With only the slightest hesitation on my part, we did just that. When we burst—and I mean burst—through the door, we were laughing louder than the band was playing. Suddenly, Kayla went totally still and quiet. I wondered at the abrupt change in her demeanor. I followed her gaze to the stage. Then I saw what she saw and heard what she heard. It was her daddy. He was singing.

She dropped my hand and ran straight for the stage. As I watched her run from me, the room changed and I felt transported into a realm of reality that was not of this world. I was completely frozen and could actually feel time slow. The band's music became a background symphony to what seemed an epic movie playing before me. Everything swelled in crescendo as my little angel climbed boldly onto the stage. The camera in my mind's eye zoomed in on her as she collected herself and walked quietly over to her daddy. Regally she stood still beside him, molding her body against his. He never stopped singing. I loved that he did not shoo her away or give her a stern don't-do-that parental look. Instead, he put his arm around her, welcoming her to the stage beside him as if it was her rightful place.

I held my breath, now realizing there was a divine purpose to this evening and it was about to be revealed. Without missing a note, my angel's daddy bent down and handed her a microphone. She acted as if she expected him to do just that, as if she were waiting on it. With the poise of a professional, she began to sing. Angelic was the only word for the sound. Though tiny in stature, she was the only star on stage. She sang without one ounce of self-consciousness, and I longed for things I had no words to express. She sang of her Creator's love and it surrounded me. For the second time that night, I felt joy in its purest form.

Overwhelmed, a tear slipped down my cheek and the joy I felt morphed into a profound sadness. An urgent prayer erupted unexpectedly from my soul. "Protect her. Do not let this world or some circumstance or cruel words steal her essence from her. Right now, she is her truest self." As I watched her, it became obvious to me that she was well loved. She was so well loved that it had birthed a confidence in her that enabled her to hug strangers, dance with abandon, and sing from a stage. She knew her role in this world—to love and be loved. "Lord, please don't let her lose that," I continued to pray. "Please don't let anyone steal that from her." As I prayed, I felt no assurance, no divine certainty that my prayer would be answered.

During my prayer, my angel finished her song and was lifted into her daddy's safe arms. He sang holding his daughter. As he continued, she put her head on his shoulder and her eyes grew so heavy that they finally closed. The now-sleeping angel, dancer, and star of the show rested her precious head on her daddy's shoulder, tired from just being her. More tears flowed down my cheeks. I cried for what would be lost in her future and for what had been lost in my past.

She is you and you were her.

These words were in me and around me. I heard them in my spirit. I was in a lonely silence when they poured into my heart. The revelation did not shock me. In that moment, there was no truer truth.

It sounds strange to say it aloud, but right then I fell in love with me—the me I used to be a long, long time ago. Another prayer erupted from my soul, but this one was all for me: "I want her back. I want to be *that* me. It was once the most natural thing in the world to live like a well-loved child, hearing the sound of your voice and loving the sound of my own. However, as I grew older, the whispers of "*stranger, stranger, danger, danger*" grew louder and caused me to hide my heart. Before I realized it, I stopped hugging strangers. I stopped dancing with abandon, and I gave up the starring role of my own life. I stopped being me—on purpose. I exchanged that role for that of an understudy in other people's lives. I guess I hoped to share their applause, never believing I would have any of my own. Please forgive me for believing that the audience of many could replace You as my audience of One. Forgive me for loving cautiously instead of extravagantly. Forgive me for protecting my heart rather than sharing it. Forgive me for not being me, the me You created me to be."

When I finished my words, a stillness and quiet peace overcame my soul.

As I ended my prayer, the band ended their song, and I was transported back to the real world. At the same time, my little angel opened her eyes and saw me across the room. As our eyes locked, I was infused with hope—hope for her and for me. She quickly left her daddy's arms and ran jumping into mine. "Can I go home with you?" she asked me very seriously. I laughed, hugging her tight and this time

I did not hesitate. Together we danced to the last of the music. I felt much younger than I had in a very long time.

My Creator used this little angel as another clue, a signpost directing me toward me and toward my destiny. Look for clues to your destiny in divine, unexpected encounters.

Your Story

Our Creator is constantly invading our ordinary, attempting to woo us to the extraordinary. Distractions, discouragement, and disappointment blind us to who we are and what we are supposed to be doing. Through my own personal journey of uncovering my identity and discovering my destiny, the lessons in this chapter helped me to really clarify and crystallize who I am and what I am supposed to be doing. What I discovered was so simple. What I am supposed to be doing was just being me—confidently—just as I had when I was child and just like my angel friend, Kayla. I thank my Creator for the introduction. She is now a part of my story.

Your life is writing a story—your story—where you are the main character and the star. Like all good stories, there are times of intense struggle, glorious adventure, pitifully ordinary days, and seasons of pain. However, when we view our lives through the lens of time, we can begin to see a common thread being woven throughout the years of our life. With the busyness and distractions of life, however, that thread is very easy to miss. I almost missed mine.

Max Lucado was also a big help.

I do not know Max personally, but I feel like I do because I have read all of his books. He is such a great storyteller. His book *Cure for the Common Life: Living in Your Sweet Spot* was another instrument my Creator used to lead me into my destiny. There is a fabulous assessment in it called S.T.O.R.Y. In it you are asked to write down very specific memories—one from childhood, one from your teen years, and one from your adult memory—when you were completely and utterly yourself. Not just happy memories but significant moments when you were simply and completely being you. Max encourages you to try to look back through the years as an observer, instead of the participant, in your own story. Consult your Creator to bring out the very memory that reflects the true essence of you. This exercise is one that requires some time and prayer. Do not be discouraged if nothing comes to you immediately—keep consulting your Creator.

Also, buy the book.

When you have remembered your moment, write a one-line summary of it, the details of how you went about doing it, and then describe what was most satisfying to you. This experience could have occurred in a ten-minute period, a day, a week, a summer, or even a year. This experience could have come from any part of your life—school, work, church, play-yard, neighborhood, home, extracurricular activities, volunteering experience, travel, or any segment of your life.

Here are the guidelines outlined in Max's book that are helpful when thinking about your moment:

- It must be important to you, though it doesn't matter what anyone else thinks of it.

- It must be a specific event or experience, not a general activity or feeling.

- It must be a specific accomplishment to you, but not a milestone such as a birthday.

- It must be specific in actions. For example, "I was good at …" or "I succeeded at …," not "I loved to play the piano" or "I loved to play softball."

When I did this exercise, I was sitting in the hospital waiting room as my husband was being taken into surgery for his injured golf elbow (sometimes our passions can land us in the hospital). As I was waiting, I was reading and thinking of memories when I was just being me. The childhood memory that first popped in my mind made me smile. It was one I had not thought about in years. It reminded me of Kayla. My first time being in a play, my first time being on a stage. I was a vegetable. I was five years old and I loved every minute of being on stage so much that I was in a play for every year afterward until I stopped being me. It did not matter if I was a pilgrim or an Indian, a farmer or a cow, a tree or a flower—I played each part as if it were opening night on Broadway.

No one had to encourage me to practice my lines. I would stand in front of a mirror for hours perfecting my performance. When I was little, I loved to watch myself in a mirror. Neither mirrors nor a stage frightened me at that age. A few years into my young acting career, the annual productions were not frequent enough to fulfill my need to perform in front of an audience, so I started writing and producing my own plays. Not only did I write the plays and produce them, I gave myself the starring role. I found the costumes for the other actors, who usually included my brother, sister, and all the neighborhood children. I assigned them their parts. I helped them rehearse their lines. I cheered them on. I advertised the event, sold tickets for the event, and shamelessly knocked on doors inviting everyone I knew and anyone I did not to come see me perform. My favorite part was seeing people come together in one place at one time for something I had a passion for—telling the story. I believed I could tell it better than anyone else could. It was all so very natural to me. I laughed at the little girl I once was. She was bossy. I recorded this memory as Max instructed in my journal.

The next memory that came to mind, and again one I had not thought of in years, was from when I was a sophomore in high school. I was leading a triple life. I had a church life, a home life, and my life as a teenager in high school. All were very different identities. I was trying so hard to be who everyone wanted me to be. It was exhausting. Looking for relief, I decided to go on our summer youth trip with my church. The location was out in my beloved wide-open spaces. I can remember lots of trees and a huge lake. I do not remember much else. I do not remember the activities we participated in, the songs we sang, or the speakers we heard, but I do remember giving up. I remember asking for and receiving forgiveness for not being me. It was a physical experience. I literally felt a heavy weight lift off my body. I felt like a new person. And for the first time in a long time, I felt like me. Now I wanted to tell everyone I knew. I wanted to shout the news from the rooftops or a stage. I got my chance. The leader of our youth group asked me to share my experience—from a stage. I had not been on one once since I had quit doing plays and quit being me. I was scared to death and at the same time so excited. Just as I had done when I was a little girl, I called everyone I knew and even some that I did not, asking them to come see me, come to hear my story. My three lives were about to be in the same room. I was about to take off my mask and unveil me. The urgency I felt was overwhelming. I wanted everyone to experience what I had, though I was not even sure what to call my experience. I felt my Creator so strongly urging me on, giving me confidence. That night came and the room was filled. Everyone I invited had come, or so it seemed. My parents were front and center. My friends as well. I took the stage. Fearless. I had no notes. I spoke my heart and people responded. I got it. For a moment during my teenage years, I had the courage to be me and I impacted others. I had tangible evidence that me being me mattered. Sadly, I remembered, it did not last for long. I could not hold on to her and I went back to being what others either wanted or needed me to be. I wrote down this memory in my journal. Sadness enveloped me in that hospital waiting room as I recorded my all regrets.

As I considered my adult story, many came to mind. In my twenties, I was the person you called to find out which bar had been designated the *happy hour* location. My nickname was *Social Director* in the company I worked for. In my thirties, I planned fundraisers for my son Austin's football team and introduced and organized Southern supper clubs in our California neighborhood. I was the fundraising director for the PTA of my younger sons' school and planned elegant galas that raised a lot of money. For six months, I trained, led, and encouraged a group of thirty-five women to prepare them to hike sixteen miles in Yosemite National Park and climb the infamous cables leading to the top of Half Dome. Again, I called everyone I knew. I assigned teams and roles. I planned for months. Cresting that summit with those women was a powerful experience. However, to date as I sat in the hospital waiting room, the greatest adult memory I had of me just being me was planning the first Courage Conference. I felt like a little girl again. I imagined the stage from where I would speak and the colors of the decorations. I shared the dream of the conference and built a team from a group of women I loved. I wrote the lines and planned the songs. I designed posters and advertised it in our small community. I worked on the flowers and the seating chart. I invited everyone I knew to join me ... and they did! When I took that stage and said aloud for the first time, "*You were created on purpose for a purpose. Do you have the courage to be you?*" I felt as if I were in a bubble where there was no time. It was all effortless. I was being me and it was so easy. It was the moment I longed for, the one I vowed would last a lifetime.

When I did this exercise, I almost fell out of my chair.

Thank you, Max, for helping me connect the dots of my story. What I discovered was truly a profound "aha" moment in my life. I almost yelled aloud to all the weary family members in the surgery waiting room with me the truth that seared into my soul.

My Destiny

Drumroll please! I love to bring people together for a purpose. I have been doing it all my life in some shape, form, or fashion.

Whatever I am doing, whatever I am passionate about (which has certainly changed throughout my life), whatever propels me into action—I want everyone I know and a multitude of people I do not to come and do it with me. I do not like parties because typically there is no purpose. I do not like games for the same reason. I would rather we all go *do* something that has meaning. I do not like to take girls trips or just hang out unless there is a task to accomplish. I could not see the contradiction before.

I love people, but I am task-oriented and driven. My heart and my passion is for people to come together for a common purpose to change the world! This is what I recorded in my journal—just in time because they were wheeling my husband out of surgery.

This nugget of truth was in every example and every story I wrote. As I reviewed the words in my journal, I realized I had not always been doing it for the right purposes. Happy hour organization was not exactly world changing. This exercise was a tremendous clue as to who I was and what I loved to do—what I was created to do and what was natural for me. It confirmed I was not a random cosmic accident. This discovery shouted that I had been created on purpose for a purpose in such a tangible way. I was stirred up, body, soul, and spirit. For years, I used my passion for my purposes, but now I sensed it was for something greater than my own. *What?* I wondered. I consulted my Creator.

What are Your plans for this planet that I am uniquely created for?

It felt like the right question. No longer was this journey about me and what I wanted. I sensed there was something unique for me to do that only I could do with a purpose much greater than I dared to ask or imagine. Revelation dawned. When we unite our purposes with our Creator's purposes, the supernatural is engaged. When we quit trying to be who we want to be and do all we want to do, then the miracles begin to happen. The power deposited within us is ignited and the angels in heaven dispatched to our aid! Now I was zip-lining. Adrenaline coursed through me. I had such a sense of urgency to be and do all I was created to. The clues were mounting up. I was ready. I could feel and almost taste my thing to do—my water-walking, giant-slaying, history-making destiny was just around the corner.

What about you? Any *aha* moments? Connecting any dots?

Seeds of desire were planted deep within each of us long before time began. From the moment we arrive on this planet, it seems there is a war to bury or kill off those dreams and desires. That is why we need courage. That is why our Creator provides us clues. They are in my story, and they are in your story. They are in the places and times you were just being you. Remember, consult your Creator.

You can be all you were created to be and do all you were created to do if you actively pursue you!

My prayer for you today is that you will rest in that knowledge. Clues are coming. You have not messed anything up. We all have regrets when we look back over our lives. Do not focus on what was lost or what you did not do. Focus on the moments when you were just being you. Your Creator has not given up on you and neither have I. Release your worries. Daily seek your Creator and look for clues.

Key Chapter Concepts to Consider :

1. Our Creator invades the ordinary to give us clues and woo us to do the extraordinary in and through us.

2. You just get to be you.

3. Live and love extravagantly not cautiously.

4. Your life is writing a story; the story provides clues.

5. Record significant moments when you were completely and utterly yourself; then looks for clues to you.

CHAPTER 18

What Breaks Your Heart?

In the year 2000, when I began asking the life-altering questions *who am I* and *what am I supposed to be doing*, I decided to pick a word to live by and focus on, instead of making the typical New Year's resolutions that I never seem to succeed at anyway. Resolutions seemed to me to be an exercise in failure that only proved my severe lack of willpower and self-control.

Thus my life altering decision to focus on a single word for the entire year. The first word I chose was *intentional* for the millennium year of 2000. It was to be my fortieth birthday year. I decided I wanted to live the next forty years differently from the last. I was determined to learn to live life intentionally instead of frantically in reaction mode. Having a word to focus on helped me do just that. I decided to become extremely focused and intentional about three things that year. The first was to intentionally tell the people in my life how much I love and appreciate them. I had a haunting dream that one day I would go to the funeral of someone I loved madly and be draped over a casket sobbing uncontrollably,

"I wish I had told them _____."

I never wanted to have to fill in that blank. I wanted the people that I loved to know they mattered to me. I wanted them to know how I felt about them. I took courage and started being intentional about showing and telling them.

My second intentional decision and focus was to daily seek my Creator—the God I had believed in my entire life—to tell me who I was and what I was supposed to be doing. Third, I wanted to be intentional in living my life on purpose for a purpose—a purpose bigger than myself. Those simple decisions and focus drastically changed my life, and I know they will change yours.

I had so much fun and I loved my word intentional for the year 2000 so much that I adopted the practice for each year thereafter. No longer was I a failure at resolutions; instead, I was a success in focus and intentionality, so much so that the people in my life began to notice.

The second year, 2001, I chose the words *prayer-filled*. That meant slowing down, becoming thoughtful, and deciding to pray about everything before reacting. It was the year I learned what it meant to have conversations with my Creator. The next year, *aware* was my word of focus, and on and on it went. Each year, around September or October, I consult my Creator about a new word, a new focus, or lesson to learn for the New Year. A*nticipation, abandon, power,* and *able* were a few I focused on. *Foundations, move forward, breakthrough,* and *harvest* were more I felt. Each word focused my days for the year and provided many lessons along the way, and some even came with divine promises, but none more than my word for the year 2011 – fulfillment.

Fulfillment.

Ah, that word, at that specific time, was music to my parched soul. I had been pregnant with dreams that felt impossible for so long—for years—and yet I chose to believe. I was even making a bit of progress. Clues were being provided as we settled into our life, making it our home in Sacramento. I continued speaking my dreams and beliefs aloud and in a dramatic fashion, and there were those who stood with me and believed. But on most days, Jake was the only one who listened. However, when I chose this word, or rather, when this word was divinely chosen for me, I believed it meant things were about to change. This whispered word meant my dreams, my desires, and my destiny was about to be revealed and fulfilled.

It was the fall of 2010. My husband had been diagnosed with cancer, and we were waiting for the surgery to be scheduled. I received the diagnosis and my word around the same time. *Fulfillment* did not seem to fit with the diagnoses. However, through the last eleven years, my Creator had taught me that my dreams and destiny often will not line up with my circumstances. I had evidence. His Word and His promises were something I could cling to and trust in the midst of a storm. So I did. I clung to peace instead of worry. Trust instead of stress. Suddenly my very hectic life and busy calendar were completely cleared as we waited for results from biopsies and surgeries. I sensed in my spirit that I was to take this time to rest and remember. It was a very strong sense I attributed to my Creator. I read a devotion that said,

Be careful to remember all your eyes have seen, do not let them slip through your heart, teach them to your children and to your children after them … remember the day it all changed.

As I read those words, I remembered the day of my journey when everything changed, when my water-walking, giant-slaying, history-making destiny was revealed. It was the day my heart was shattered into a million pieces, and I felt I was to remember and write it all down.

It's a Home

It's a home. It's a home. It's a home. Those words were whispered to my heart one Sunday morning as I sat in church, as I had for most every Sunday morning of my entire life. Being raised in Mississippi, the Bible Belt, this habit was established early in my life, but in all those years of church attendance, never once did I walk through those doors expecting my life to change. However, on Sunday, July 22, 2007, my life did just that.

I sat in the huge auditorium, waiting for the service to begin, engulfed by three thousand people. I did not know a single one of them aside from my two teenage sons who sat beside me. My husband was playing golf. I was feeling lonely and melancholy that particular day. We had been in Sacramento for a year, fighting to survive. We had lost our home, and we missed our friends and the comfortable life we had built on the Bay Area. Hanging on to my identity and destiny during this time was extremely difficult. However, I took courage and chose to believe—daily, in spite of my feelings and circumstances. The whispered words of my Creator kept me going. *"Don't reduce the size of your dreams and desires to accommodate your present circumstances. They won't fit."* Daily, I vowed to try.

Thank God I did. Because on this day, everything suddenly changed, everything suddenly made sense, and I suddenly knew what I was supposed to do.

It's a home.

There was a guest speaker at church that Sunday morning. Don Brewster. Although a preacher, he did not preach. Instead, he told of how his own heart was broken and then recalibrated by God over an issue I had never heard about: sex trafficking.

With his words, he painted a picture I did not want to see. Children being sold for sex in the world I live in.

He told of children in Cambodia, as young as five years old, who were systematically sold to men for sex. Sold as if they were a commodity with no value, no feelings or purpose. My body was literally racked with sobs, much to my sons' embarrassment. At one point, I looked around the room to see if I was the only one pierced by the images created in my mind's eye. Everyone looked so normal. I felt I was the only one of the thousands attending that day who could hear these children's cries, feel the trauma they endured, and see the pain in their eyes.

I could feel my heart breaking, violently ripping inside of me. I doubted I would ever be the same.

It's a home. I continued to hear this whispered to my spirit as Don began to tell how his own life had changed when he learned of the plight of these Cambodian children. When he and his wife, Bridget, learned of this hideous crime against children from a TV show they watched, they knew they had to do something. So they did what any of us would do with the same knowledge (*not,* as my teenagers would say). They quit their jobs, sold everything they owned, and moved to Cambodia to start a home for children rescued from the sex slave trade—all with absolutely no idea just how to do that. He made it sound so simple.

It's a home. At this point in the service, the atmosphere dramatically changed. Instead of horror being recounted over and over, there was hope being delivered in large doses. Don began to tell stories of what a difference a home, and a family, makes in the lives of these vulnerable yet invisible children. He read stories of children who had the privilege of living there, children who had names, who had beautiful faces, and who I knew had a unique destiny.

It's a home. I wrote those words over and over on my church bulletin. The stories Don told of tangible restoration, the stories of hope and of transformation, were ones I believed God was writing, and they caused a seismic shift inside of me. I wanted to be a part of that restoration story. I wanted to bring people together for that purpose. I wanted to shout it out loud that these children were created on purpose for a purpose. I could hardly remain silent. The stories Don told reminded me of the ones I had heard as a small child going to church on Sunday. It was the story of God doing extraordinary things through ordinary people. Don said he was one. I wanted to be another. I realized it was a story our Creator wanted to write on each of our lives … including the lives of these vulnerable children.

It's a home.

For days after that church service I prayed, "Cambodia? You want me to go to Cambodia?" I really did not think my husband, in our current financial and emotional situation, was going to agree to moving our family to Cambodia. In fact, I was certain of it. So instead, I wrote the biggest donation check that would clear our bank account to the Brewster's non-profit organization, thinking that would satisfy the ache in my heart and maybe even be the prompting of my Creator. It did not work. I still cried for weeks. I literally cried for all the children around the world being sold to strangers by the parents who were supposed to love and protect them. I cried as if they were my own daughters. When I confided to a friend that I thought I was going crazy with grief for children I had never met, who felt like my own, she told me that she believed God was letting me feel His heart for these precious little ones. "It's unbearable," I sobbed.

Eventually, I had a fight with my Creator over this hideous issue of selling children for sex. "You could make this stop. You could take it off the table. Make this issue, the issue of selling children, cease!" I angrily demanded.

I felt a whispered response to my heart: *What age would that be? Five years old? Ten? Is it okay for a fifteen-year-old to be tortured, raped, and sold for sex? A twenty-five-year-old?* I could see this arguing with my Maker was going nowhere, so I shouted from the depths of my soul, "JUST DO SOMETHING!" And before I had time to take a breath, He said to me, *Why don't you?*

That was a holy moment.

Time stood still.

It's a home.

"I'm just a mom," I whined.

Good, because that is just what they need—a mom, a family. These are your daughters, the daughters you have longed for. Find them, build them a home, call them family.

I gasped. These were my daughters. Everything became clear. My dreams were about to be fulfilled. Courage House, it's a home for children rescued from sex trafficking and I was to build it. I quickly needed to become an expert in what broke my heart.

Do Something!

As the weeks and months of 2007 came and went, I continued to be brokenhearted for children I had never met but who felt like my own. Though I daily battled through our family's difficult financial situation, the desire to *do something* for these kids did not diminish but accelerated in my spirit. During the beginning of 2008, I sought direction, answers, and wisdom from the place all God-fearing people go … Google. I began researching the words "sex trafficking" and "human trafficking," expecting to see details of this horrific crime in faraway countries I had never visited. I was shocked to the core of my being when the words appeared on my screen: Sacramento.

Sacramento? My home? My city? Through my research, I learned children were being sold for sex right in my own backyard—in my city, my state, and in my country. While the reality of children being sold in Cambodia broke my heart, the news that they were being sold in my own backyard outraged me and propelled me into action. This time I did not have to take courage; I was angry and bold.

Anger was my fuel and energy.

I remembered the Enneagram assessment I had taken back in the early years of my identity boot camp, and anger had been identified as a facet of my personality. I remembered being confused because I really did not get angry with much. However, as I made a careful assessment of who I was, I learned my Maker had deposited anger inside me when I encountered injustices that required change. Up until that point of my life, I just had not encountered much that you would call injustice.

Now I got it. At that moment, I believed with everything I was that I had been created on purpose *for this purpose* because I was totally confident in my identity and I knew rescuing these children, my daughters, was my destiny.

Everything made sense. My life was at the pivotal point of convergence—when everything in your life lines up. When every experience, every job, every conversation, every assessment, and even every struggle makes sense. I knew what I had to do. But even more exciting, I knew what I was created to do. I had been divinely equipped for it my entire life. My journey of purpose during the last seven years served to show me how. I am a mom—a nurturer. I am a cheerleader—an encourager. I am a conduit—a leader to gather people for a passionate purpose. I am a communicator—a loud voice angry at injustice. I am an activist—I have to do something. Though still extremely ordinary, I *am* a water walker, giant slayer, and history maker.

These invisible children were my long-awaited daughters, and my purpose at this point in my life was to build them a home and call them family. My life and my journey had led me to this moment. I felt like I was standing on the ledge of an airplane and someone was screaming, *"JUMP!"*

So I did.

"We are going to build a Courage House in every city around the world that needs one ... starting with my city, Sacramento, California."

It's a home.

It sounded so simple and at the same time impossible. However, I felt compelled to say it aloud to anyone who would listen.

I had already started a non-profit organization with two friends of mine, called *Courage to Be You, Inc.*, before I left the Bay Area. We thought we would be producing Courage Conferences and encouraging individuals around the world to uncover their identity and discover their destiny. I believed the children I had heard about needed to do just that. I just had no idea how to bring it about.

When I eventually met Bridget Brewster, Pastor Don's wife, I asked her, "How? What do you do? How do you start?"

She gave me the perfect answer: *One step at a time.*

So that was what I did. I picked up the phone and courageously called a woman who worked at the state capitol in California and who had authored a state-funded report regarding human trafficking in our state. I asked if it were true. She said yes. All throughout the report I read, it stated there was a lack of services for victims and that restoration homes were needed. I told her I would build one. Imagine my surprise when she invited me to a meeting at the capitol.

Now I needed courage because my knees were knocking.

The state capitol? The fear of embarrassment raised its ugly head, but I squashed it with words of belief. I may have been scared to death, but I was walking on water. I did not have any money, much less a college degree or a staff, but I had a vision and finally the knowledge of what I was on this planet to do. However, I had to stop looking at the waves crashing up around my ankles or I would sink—fast. So I took my friend Terry's advice and remembered that I was a child of God. So I started acting like it. I dressed in my best, most professional outfit, did my hair and makeup, and then got in my car and drove downtown for my first meeting at the state capitol. I truly felt like a country bumpkin coming to town, accompanied by my Southern accent still intact after fifteen years in California. I felt a little crazy.

As I drove, I made a deal with my Creator. I would go to that meeting, but I was not going to say a word. I was going to be quiet because I did not want to look as stupid as I felt. These were the experts; I was a novice. I knew my place, but I must have forgotten who I was. (Me, be quiet?) Still I tried. For two hours I listened as experts, professionals, and government officials talked about the enormous problem of human trafficking and child sex trafficking in our nation and in our state. It seemed like everyone was very familiar with the problem. And they even knew the solution. It's a home. However, no one seemed able to make a decision or authorize the funding and building of one. I could not stand it any longer. Without a conscious thought, I jumped up in the middle of that room, interrupted the conversation, and confidently told them that I was going to build a home for these children—me and my non-profit organization, Courage to Be You, Inc. (They had no idea I was the only volunteer at the time.) Not satisfied, I went on to say that, in fact, God's people in this city were going to build the home because it was our responsibility. (They had no idea that I knew no one in this town.) I explained that once these good people knew children were being sold for sex, the money would coming pouring in and we would have plenty of beds for children in need. Then I sat down, wondering where that boldness and those words came from. I fought feelings of embarrassment, choosing instead to trust truth. I was created to make this happen.

No one said a word. They did not even look at me. They just began talking again about the problem as if I had not said a word.

When the meeting came to an end, I ran to my car in my high heels. I cried all the way home. I felt like the village idiot. Yes, I had forgotten that crazy was a part of this journey. I felt sorry for myself and did not tell anyone about this experience. However, I was getting madder. I screamed at my Maker, "What was that?" Silence.

That was February 2008. Haunted by the idea of my daughters being raped, abused, and tortured night after night, I finally got over myself and, when I saw an article in the newspaper about the issue, summoned the courage to pick up the phone to call the Sacramento Police Department. Once again, I was walking on water trying to keep from sinking. I dialed the number and asked for the department that dealt with crimes against children. I was told to hold. I had a strong urge to hang up.

But before I did, Detective Haun introduced himself. Detective? He sounded way above my pay grade.

With all the courage I could muster, and in my most professional voice, I said, "My name is Jenny Williamson and my non-profit, Courage to Be You, is building homes for minor victims of sex trafficking around the world. Do you think the Sacramento area is in need of one?" I sounded crazy to myself! However, this stranger did not seem to think so. He took me dead seriously, asked if I would like to meet an officer who was working directly with these young victims, and then replied, "Thank you. We need that home. How soon can you build it?" I had no answer, which, with water-walking, giant-slaying, history-making destinies, you do not have to. Whew.

He gave me the officer's name and phone number. I called her and arranged to meet her for coffee. Officer Pam, I called her. I shared my dream of Courage House, a home for these young victims, and she told me about the kids she was attempting to recover. She said there were those who called them throwaways. With tears in her eyes, she said to me, "I often wonder who these kids were supposed to have been." Ah! She got it. They *were* created on purpose for a purpose. I was heartbroken all over again and getting madder by the minute. With no safe place to go when rescued, Officer Pam had taken them into her home and was using her own money to buy them food and clothes. (Shhh, don't tell anyone—we do not want to get her in trouble.) As we talked, she confirmed, "We need a home. They are going to die in this life." She did not think I was crazy; instead, she asked if I would like to meet the FBI Innocence Lost Task Force leader, who had a mandate from the federal government to rescue these vulnerable children and put away their perpetrators. I did not hesitate—my answer was yes. I arranged another coffee meeting to meet FBI Special Agent Minerva. I wondered at her name. It sounded like someone's old aunt. When she walked through the doors of our coffee shop, she was anything but old. When I learned the meaning of her name, it all made sense: goddess of war. She was fighting a war to rescue these vulnerable kids.

When I told her the dream of Courage House, not only did she believe me, but she agreed to go around town speaking with me, telling others of this crime against our children. To understand these children and their unique needs, I started hanging out with vice cops and FBI agents. I learned all I could about this vulnerable population. I was actively and passionately becoming an expert in what broke my heart.The more I learned, the more my heart broke for them. I made more phone calls, to social workers, probation officers, and juvenile justice judges, because I learned that most of the kids being rescued were runaways and or in the foster care system, and many of them were hurt by the people who were supposed to protect them. Did I mention I was getting madder?

Finally, I got the courage to email Pastor Don and Bridget Brewster, asking them how they had built a home for children rescued from sex trafficking in Cambodia, and hoping they would have some kind of a blueprint I could follow, because I actually had no idea what I was doing and how I was going to do it. In the meantime, I continued to have coffee with complete strangers, shouting to anyone who would listen that my organization was going to build Courage House, a home for these children. Then I told the Brewsters via email that I wanted to do in Sacramento what they had done in Cambodia. To my utter delight, they agreed to meet with me. Their yes was such a great encouragement. I shudder to think what would have happened if they were too busy to meet with me.

I met them at our church, where they were being interviewed by the local newspaper. When Bridget saw me, she grabbed the reporter and photographer and ran over to me. As she approached me, I could hear her enthusiastically telling them both, "This is Jenny Williamson, and she is going to do what we have done in Cambodia—build a home for children rescued from sex trafficking right here in Sacramento." I almost fell on the floor. I was speechless as the reporter asked to interview me and the photographer took pictures of me. All I could think about was how I had not even told my husband yet about this population of children.

This was such a crazy time in my life. Things were happening so fast that I could not keep up. In the midst of all that was happening with regard to sex trafficking, a friend of mine had moved to Africa to work at an orphanage there. She told me that there was so much land and they just needed someone to come plant a garden. I volunteered my dad without him knowing it. He said yes and started to walk on water at sixty-nine years of age. This trip was his first of many to Africa to plant gardens, build churches, and feed widows and orphans. My mom joined him. A year later, I was invited to join them in Tanzania, Africa to produce and speak at a Courage Conference. I finally had a passport. My little girl-dream of traveling the world to tell people of their loving Creator was about to be fulfilled. While I was there, I was given a building out in the bush. I wondered what I needed with a building in Africa. I did not have much time to ponder the thought because when my plane touched back down in Sacramento, there was another article in the newspaper on child sex trafficking.

My meetings were increasing and I was running around town like a chicken with my head cut off, passionately telling strangers in coffee shops about the needs of these vulnerable victims. I was drinking so much coffee that I was beginning to think I could fly. Finally, I decided to invite everyone who had expressed a desire to see this home built, into one room with decision makers to formally and publically announce that we were going to build this home. I invited the Brewsters to speak about what a difference the home in Cambodia had made to children there. I asked the local police department and FBI task force to detail for this group of community leaders the incredible number of young children who were being sold in our city. To my utter amazement, sixty people showed up. Judges, lawyers, child welfare workers, probation officers, lawmakers, and many others, including the local newspaper. I again declared that we were going to build a home for children who have been trafficked for sex. The reporter again took my picture and asked me for my office number. Since I did not have one, I gave her my home phone.

The next morning our phone began to ring at 5:00 a.m. The reporter printed a full-page article in the *Sacramento Bee* about the issue of trafficking and my dream to build a home. There was my picture and home photo plastered across the *Sacramento Bee*. Over two hundred people called or emailed me on that day, starting at 5:00 a.m. much to my husband's surprise, saying, "We want to help build the home."

These two hundred people, who on that day decided to read the newspaper and were moved by their Maker to call or email me, were the answer to the prayers I had been praying to my Creator: *How? When? Who? Where are your people?*

With that one newspaper article, He sent me an army.

He also sent me something else—evidence that this home was needed.

Of those two hundred phone calls, I received three from women who identified themselves as prostitutes—their word, not mine. I was so shocked that each of them said the very same thing to me: "Please build the home. It is too late for me, but if there had been a place when I was a teen on the streets, maybe my life would be different. Please build this home. All they need is someone to believe in them."

Over and over, I began to hear the words *believe in me, believe in me. Who would I be if you believed in me?*

It was as if I could hear the voices of the children crying out in the night. My heart was literally breaking, and I believed I heard my Creator whisper, *who would they be if they believed in Me?*

Passion, purpose, and urgency filled my spirit. These homes must be built, these children must be rescued. They just need a family and someone to believe in them.

On the same day of the newspaper article and subsequent phone calls, Officer Pam called me and wanted me to meet her for lunch. She had a sixteen-year-old who had been repeatedly trafficked for sex that she wanted to introduce me to, a young girl she had befriended. I immediately said no. I had purposefully avoided this very thing. How could I look into the eyes of a child who had been tortured in this way and just say, "Hang on. I'm praying for you. I have a dream to build a home, but I have not idea how it is going to happen."?

"No, thank you," I said. However, police officers can be very persuasive—and they carry guns. So I went to the Chevy's by the river to meet this child. I was so nervous. She looked like any teenager I had met. She could have been a friend of my sons. She knew I knew her story. Prompted by my cop friend, I told her mine and the dream of Courage House. She listened, and I had no idea what she was thinking. I asked if there were such a place, would she come. Without looking me in the eye, she just nodded her head. I tried to engage her in conversation, so I asked what these girls would need most at Courage House. When I paused for her answer, she was staring at her uneaten food. Then without hesitation, she looked into my eyes and said, "They just need someone to believe in them."

Believe in me, believe in me. Who would I be if you believed in me?

I tried to answer all the phones calls and emails I received on that day. It took weeks, and all during that time I continued to be haunted by the words *believe in me.*

One afternoon as I was waiting for one of my coffee dates, I was writing the words on paper and whispered a prayer, *Are these words a song?* Inspiration flooded my soul. We need a song, a video to tell the story of these children. Their stories were so horrific that it was difficult to find the words to explain. *Yes, a song, that is what we need.* Then I laughed, because I cannot carry a tune in a bucket much less write a song. I wondered who would write this song and film this video. Maybe it would be someone else's destiny.

My coffee date that day was Stephanie Midthun, a woman whose husband pastored a local church. As she sat down, she saw my scribbled words on a scratch paper.

"What's that?" she inquired.

"A song," I laughed and told her the story.

She smiled confidently. "I'm a songwriter." Of course she was. She went on to tell me how she had raised tens of thousands of dollars for an orphanage in Africa. Africa, hmm. I told her I had just been given a building there.

I ripped the paper from my notebook and asked her to write a song called *Believe in Me*. She agreed. Days later, I cried as I read the lyrics, and in January 2009 on National Anti-Human Trafficking Day, I had the privilege to hear Christina Smit, a fifteen-year-old, sing the words written by Stephanie, inspired by three women who had no hope for their own home but who longed for someone to *believe in me*.

That song, and later a phenomenal music video also titled "Believe in Me," written and produced by a young filmmaker Aaron Schnobrich, who volunteered all his time for the project, became the vehicle our organization used to tell the story of children who were being raped, abused, tortured, and sold for sex in our very own backyard. The newspaper article brought a team, an army of people to the organization, Courage to Be You, Inc., and we all vowed to build the home. All our hearts were broken over these young ones. We began to challenge people to do what they loved to do for these children, and they did. We were especially blessed by the local music community and bands like The Reel, The Music Room, and performing artist Chaya, who donated songs and helped produce a music CD to raise funds for the home. We then began doing Courage Concerts to be a voice for these voiceless children. People responded.

As I write these words to you, my heart begins to pound. It was such a special time in my life. I had gone from being alone with my dreams to now daily working with an incredible volunteer team. Not one person received a dime in pay. We were all volunteers and vowed not to take a cent for ourselves until that home was built. Our faith was the fuel. At the time, we all thought we were a little crazy and out on the proverbial limb. However, we were walking on water and loving every minute of it. We all had the courage to be who we were created to be and encouraged everyone we met to do the same.

When I came to understand my Creator wanted me to build this home, I kept asking all the logical logistical questions like, *Where? When? How?* When I got no answer or sense of direction, I decided to wait and just believe it would all be brought to me in time. I figured that anyone can hire a realtor, find land, and engage a banker to finance it.

Soon there was a choir of voices asking the same questions. "Where are you looking for property?" they would ask.

My response would be, "I'm not looking."

"Have you hired a realtor?"

"No," would be my response. I wanted a story to wow the world. I wanted to be an example of how God uses ordinary people to do extraordinary things. So I waited, believing that my Creator wanted to do the impossible for these vulnerable, abused children and that He wanted to do it through me and the small team of individuals that made up Courage to Be You, Inc., now called Courage Worldwide.

One year later, I received the address to Courage House.

I was standing on a stage at a Courage Conference encouraging the crowd to dream big, impossible dreams by challenging them with the question *do you have the courage to be you?* I was also telling them about my pursuit of purpose and how it led me to a group of vulnerable children. "We need fifty acres of land in a rural community far away from downtown. We need wide-open spaces at the base of the mountains. I can hear running water, and I see horses. There is a white picket fence around the property," I boldly declared from the stage.

After the conference was over, a woman walked up to me with tears running down her cheeks and said, "I have your home. It is fifty acres in a rural area. It is at the base of the foothills, and there is a creek that runs right down the middle of the property. There are horses and, yes, there is a white fence around the entire property. And it is for sale."

We both cried. I was not even sure if she was real—maybe she was an angel. I looked for the property that night on the Internet when I got home. I wept as the wide-open spaces came into view. It was exactly what I had imagined. To see what I had only dreamed was indescribable. My first thought was, *I'm not crazy.* I went to visit the property during the next week, and I knew in my spirit that this was the Promised Land, the address of the first Courage House. This would be the place young girls would come to find healing and restoration. This would be the place where I welcomed my daughters home.

Though it looked impossible, I believed. It was my destiny.

I knew that I was going to have to call on all the lessons I had learned during boot camp. The property cost over $1,100,000 and we only had $10,000 in the bank. I guessed it was time to find a realtor as crazy as I was! My Creator was once again asking me to trust Him and not play it safe. He was asking me to walk on water, to risk being thought of as crazy.

The realtor found me.

The weekend before we met, I spoke at a small church of about two hundred people in the Lake Tahoe area. I told them we live in a world where children are sold for sex. I told them about the property. I asked them to pray for me. Immediately after the service, they held an emergency board meeting and then handed me a check for $40,000. This was real! I now had $50,000 in the bank for when I made the offer on a $1,100,000 piece of property.

I met the realtor the next day and asked how he felt about making an offer on a piece of property when said organization only had $50,000 in the bank. He laughed and said, "Sure." Though I was scared to death, I signed the contracts, making an offer on a piece of property that I believed would one day be home to children who did not have one. I felt a little crazy.

Our offer was refused.

I was shocked. Really, I was. They had taken an offer that included $600,000 as a down payment. I went back to my Creator, trying to determine what just happened. *Fight for it.* So we did. We fought for these children. We continued to hold Courage Concerts and Courage Runs and any other type of fundraiser we could think of to raise the funds to bring these children home. At the same time, a courageous young women I met agreed by faith to go to Tanzania, Africa and begin getting the building we had been given there ready to welcome children. We now saw the need for a Courage House there; children were being sold for sex in the area where we had been given a building. Lauren was the young woman's name. She is a true water walker.

I received a phone call from our realtor. "The offer fell through. The owners want to know if you still would like the home and the land."

"Yes!"

"How much money do you have now?"

"Three hundred fifty thousand dollars." Our events were proving successful, and the community responded generously in the worst economic year since the Great Depression.

We made another crazy offer. No response from the owners. We kept praying and kept raising awareness and funds. The offer expired.

Another four months passed and the realtor called again. "The owners have another offer on the property and wanted to know if you wanted to make one also."

"Yes!"

"How much money do you have now?"

"Six hundred fifty thousand dollars—still very short of one hundred thousand."

It was late 2009, almost 2010, and the economic forecast was still dismal for the United States. Many people said our quest was impossible in this climate and that there was no way we could pull this off. They were right—but we believed God could.

We made another offer. We waited, we prayed, and we believed. The results were not ours to produce. We had done our part. We had persevered and participated in the process. We were at peace.

The phone rang on February 2, 2010. "The owner will accept your offer and is willing to finance the remainder of the balance for you over the next seven years, with a twenty-five-year amortization. Do you want to accept this offer?" the realtor asked.

"Yes! Oh, yes!" I screamed. I sang, I danced, and I called everyone I knew. I wept and sobbed over the miracle that not only I had not watched but I had participated in.

The simple dream became a reality. We had a home. Well, actually we had two homes. We purchased the fifty acres of land, a house, and barn for the first U.S.A. Courage House, in a rural area outside of Sacramento, California, and, additionally, we were given horses to begin our equestrian program. We also leased a building for free in Tanzania, Africa for what was to become the first International Courage House.

We had the homes. Now we needed the girls.

They arrived two months later, one eighteen and one twenty-three. One found me on the Internet when she saw the music video *Believe in Me* and emailed me, encouraging me to build the home, all the while believing it was too late for her. The other stalked me at our concerts and events. She finally confronted me in the bathroom at one venue and said, "I am one of your daughters."

Both called me "mom" without hesitation and, in the most childlike manner, assumed that since they were my daughters that my husband was their dad and my sons their brothers. I laugh and tell everyone that they came for lunch, then for dinner. They came for a weekend and then longer at Thanksgiving. They stayed two weeks at Christmas and a month in February. Somewhere along the way, we called them family.

My Creator fulfilled the dreams and desires He placed in the heart of a child long before time began. I had married a man I loved and birthed sons, had spoken on a stage, was writing a book, was given daughters, and had traveled to a faraway place telling the people there of a Creator who created them on purpose for a purpose. My mom had been right. California was to be my mission field, but it was also the place I would also remember who I was and have the courage to be and do all I was created to. It was the place where my dreams and destiny were fulfilled.

ou too have place to stand and a mission to fulfill. What breaks your heart. What is unbearable for you to contemplate. I believe things, those issues are clues to what you are to impact, what you life is to affect. Become an expert in what breaks your heart. Use your voice as a trumpet. Shout it out loud then take one crazy, courageous step towards your destiny. Like me, it may just be sending an email or making a phone call. Do not hesitate. Just do something.

Key Chapter Concepts to Consider :

1. Chose to live intentionally.

2. Pay attention to what breaks your heart - do not run from it, run towards it.

3. Become an expert in the issue.

4. Be a part of the solution.

5. Consult your creator for the how.

CHAPTER 19

Quitting Isn't an Option

I was walking off a stage at Green Valley Church in Placerville, California after giving an emotional talk on the reality of child sex slavery in our country. Pastor Ken followed me to wrap up the evening and ask for an offering. He stood still and silent on the stage. I could feel his emotions and watched as he struggled to control them. Silence enveloped the room, and you could hear people crying. We were all overcome with the images and stories of young girls whose bodies were being ravaged nightly while we slept in our safe homes.

Finally the pastor looked up and passionately declared, "The church needs to go straight to hell!"

We were all in stunned shock.

"Because that is where these children are—in hell."

He was right. These children, my daughters, are living in hell. These children are not going to come knocking on our doors asking for help. Someone is going to have to rescue them. Someone is going to have to fight for them, figuratively and literally. I learned that my destiny would require me to be one of those somebodies. It was going to require me to take bold action.

Your destiny is going to require you to do the same. Someone is waiting for you to have the courage to be you. Someone is waiting for you to do something.

My daughter courageously did. Thought she was once a victim of this horrendous crime, she did not offer it as an excuse to do nothing. She got her college degree, obtained a teaching certificate, taught her baby sisters at Courage House, and now works for Courage Worldwide rescuing more children and is also a secret agent at Starbucks where she encourages customers to join the fight to stop this abuse and torture of children.

If she has to, she will go into enemy territory. Will you? Will you be an agent of change?

Acting Boldly

We need ordinary men and women who will act boldly.

Simply start by making a careful assessment of who you are. Then you will figure out what you are supposed to be doing. The discovery of your true identity will proceed fulfilling your destiny. Choose to believe you are a child of God—a loving Creator who created you on purpose for a purpose before time began. Choose to believe, in spite of your feelings and in spite of your circumstances. Vow to achieve your water-walking, giant-slaying, history-making destiny.

Yes, you will be scared—but only in the beginning. Begin to anticipate and look forward to the day when you are not afraid anymore. It will come. Something will change. You will be fearless. You will become bold.

The dictionary defines **bold** as the following: *"to trust, to be confident, secure, sure, to be frank in speech, confident in demeanor, outspoken, blunt, assured, to be bold, to be free, open and plain, commanding, break the silence, courageous, daring in all things and in all matters, in speaking and acting."*

I love this. It really is a picture of what it means to be living out your destiny.

Boldness comes making courageous choices over and over again. Listening to your Creator, feeling a bit crazy, facing impossible situations, feeling ordinary but doing the extraordinary. You have been given the honor of participating in the process. You have never felt so alive. You now have something you can live for, but you also have something you would die for.

You are fearless. You are bold. That makes you dangerous. Now there is no way you will ever quit. It is not an option, because lives are at stake.

I end this book as I began it—telling you that you have a purpose, an important part to play on this planet. There is something for you to do that only *you* can do. And if you do not do it, it will never get done. Your unique contribution matters—and it will matter to countless people if you quit.

Your destiny may be tied to loving and believing in someone when they cannot love or believe in themselves. *It matters if you quit!* Your destiny may involve consistent and persistent parenting of a child who struggles to learn. *It matters if you quit.* Your destiny may require you to build, write, or create something tangible to share with this world. *It matters if you quit.* Your destiny may be a discovery that literally saves lives, or it may involve giving a hug or writing a note that makes another feel that life is worth living. *It matters if you quit.* Your destiny may be one of persevering in prayer for someone's safety, salvation, or healing. *It matters if you quit.*

You being you matters. Much is depending upon you having the courage to be you. Quitting is not an option.

"I would literally be dead if you had quit or said no. Thank you for having the courage to be you."

My adoptive daughters have spoken those words to me on numerous occasions since I met them four years ago; both had pasts that involved extreme sexual abuse and exploitation. Loving them and calling them family felt like the most natural thing in the world to me. Ten years ago when I first heard the words,

"Do you have the courage to be you?"

I never contemplated their impact on another person. Now I do. After hearing my daughter's story, now I do.

Here is the story of a girl who once called Courage House home—one of my daughters:

For most of my life, I have been afraid. I was born into a family who worshipped evil. I was born even though my birth mother tried to abort me. From my earliest memories, I knew I was unwanted and that my own mother hated me.

All the adults in my life seemed to hate me, even though I did everything they asked, hoping it would make them love me. But I learned very quickly their love came at a price.

I was taught a religion that was full of rituals accompanied by torment. I went to "church" often and sometimes we even had church at our house. I have seen and experienced things that no one should, especially a child. My birth parents prayed over me and asked that fear and pain be my friends so I would be silent and not talk about the torment and torture.

Until I was twenty-three years old, I never talked without permission.

On my sixth birthday, my birth mother sold me to my uncle with my father's knowledge and consent. I was told, "If you love me, you will do this." So I did.

My uncle told me he owned me, and I believed him. I was owned by something dark and evil that shaped my life for many, many years.

As a child, I was raped, cut, burned, beaten, stabbed, and used in pornography night after night. I was locked in a yellow bedroom that was my own private hell. I never dreamed I would ever leave, but at the same time I silently hoped that a new family would find me and love me.

In the daylight hours, I was let out of my room to go to school and ballet class. I learned to read. My teachers told me I was smart. School became my only escape besides the drugs I was given. Men continued to come in and out of my bedroom at night. Sometimes I fell asleep in class or at the library. It seems strange to me now as an adult that no one ever asked why I was always hungry, tired, bruised, or scared. No one asked why I stopped talking.

I became a child without a voice. Not talking was easier than enduring the punishment of being left alone in the dark for days without food. I thought my life was a mistake and that I was invisible.

At seven, I started traveling to different cities in the U.S. and then to countries around the world with my uncle. He said he wanted me to meet his "friends." Now I was locked in basements and attics where men visited and spoke in languages I didn't understand. I was taught to smile and make them happy or I would have to endure more punishment. We traveled two weeks out of every month. This became my normal.

Every year, the abuse got more hideous and intense. But still I held out hope to be rescued and to find a family who loved me.

When I was fourteen, I met a pastor and his family at a grocery store after school. I was hungry and was contemplating stealing something to eat. This family noticed me and talked with me. They were so kind. They invited me to come on a retreat with them that weekend. I thought I had been saved. I jumped in their minivan aware that this rash decision might get me killed. I went anyway.

The pastor's wife asked me if I needed to call home or get a change or clothes or a toothbrush. I told her that my mom and uncle would never let me go away for the weekend, so either I go with her or I go with them. That was the most I had talked to another human being who wasn't asking me to take my clothes off in a very long time. She stopped asking questions and started driving a little faster.

That weekend I heard words I had never heard before but went straight to my dry heart. I was told I was a wonder, a masterpiece. I was told that I was loved and planned. Though I wanted to believe, I couldn't believe they were meant for me. So I just took advantage of the uninterrupted sleep and the food. I studied the stars and contemplated questions that I thought had no answers.

After the weekend was over, I went back home to my uncle. I decided hope was not for me. Life continued as it always had. By now I believed what I had been told—this was my destiny.

One night, quite unexpectedly, I heard a whisper that wasn't evil—it was around my sixteenth birthday. I believed it was God. He told me that He still calmed storms and He could calm the one inside of me. But

I couldn't see the storm ending or if I wanted it to. I decided that responding to the whisper was too risky. Dying felt easier. I literally begged to die. But "they" wouldn't let me.

When I turned eighteen, my life changed dramatically. My uncle died instead of me!

I was free at last. My uncle had left me some money, so I decided to run away and go to college. I knew if I stayed that my family would only sell me again. I was smart and I could read. College made sense. A new life. A new city. I wanted to be somebody different—someone not like me.

But darkness was waiting.

Almost immediately, I met a man who told me I was beautiful. He told me I was special and that he could love me. His words filled up all my empty spaces in my heart, and I believed every word he spoke. He was the very first person I told about my childhood.

And that was the beginning of a new hell that lasted almost four years. My childhood could not compare to life with him. But he told me that my childhood had prepared me well for his plans. He too sold me to any man who would pay his price in cities here in the U.S. and ones around the world. I stopped believing in rescue, in a family, and in good. Now he said I was worthless and that no one would love me. I believed that too and just did what I was told.

But it seems a divine plan was pursuing me.

In September 2009, I saw a video on Facebook called "Believe in Me," produced by Courage Worldwide, showing the life of a young girl being "trafficked" and the vision to build young victims a home, believe in them, and call them family.

I was shocked as I watched. The video was showing my life. The men, the locked doors, the drugs, the torture, and terror. I felt afraid and vulnerable. I didn't know anyone knew. I hated the life I was leading, but seeing it on the screen made me want to run, to leave, to cry, or scream.

But where would I go? I had evidence no one cared about me. But after seeing that video, I just couldn't stay.

That video had such an impact on my life; I decided to send the founder of the organization, who produced the video, an email. I told Jenny that when I watched that video for the first time, I felt like someone saw me, that someone knew me, and they cared. I told her I had been in an unsafe situation but now I was going to do something different. I told her that I believed it was too late for me to live in one of her Courage Houses, but I encouraged her to build the homes for other children like me.

I did not think I'd hear back from her. I lived on the East Coast, and she was on the West. I did not tell her in that email that daily I contemplated death, that I had no plan for my life or any idea where to go. Surprisingly, she and a lady in her office emailed me back. They tried to encourage me, but the pull of the past was too strong.

I graduated from college, then I walked back into hell. For two weeks I was surrounded by darkness. Again, I wanted to die, but every time I contemplated it, I would hear the "Believe in Me" song in my head and in my heart.

Believe in me, believe in me ... I am longing for my captive heart to be free.

It was the longing of my heart. Again, I knew I had to leave. I was not numb any longer. I could not keep living like this. That song had given me hope, and it was growing daily. Leaving his house for the last time was hard. I left without shoes in the middle of the night in a rainstorm. But because of that choice, God could finally start to calm the storm inside of me. A few weeks later, I called Jenny on the phone for the very first time. I told her that I had left for good. She asked me what my plan was. I told her I'd call her back when I figured it out.

When I did, I called her Mom. I guess it's weird to call someone Mom whom you've never met before, but it felt right. As soon as the words were out of my mouth, I was embarrassed, but she laughed and said, "God told me I would have daughters one day." We continued to talk and build a relationship. One day she asked me if I wanted to come home.

On May 27, 2010, I got on a plane to fly to California and to call people "family" that I had never met before and move into a house I had never seen. Courage House. My home. God fulfilled the little-girl prayer of my heart that I would be rescued, have a new family and a place to sleep where no one came into my bedroom late at night.

However, I have found so much more. I have found freedom and hope and a future. I have found that long before time began I was created on purpose for a purpose—all because people simply believed in me and called me family. All because of one woman's fight for her identity and destiny; all because she had the courage to be and do all God created her to. All because she decided to be a voice for the voiceless, build them homes, and call them family. Jenny, my mom, gave me permission to speak. Now I can help other girls discover their identity and fulfill their destiny.

That is why you cannot quit. Someone is praying a prayer and waiting on God, and *He is waiting on you.*

I will ask you one last time,

Do you have the courage to be you?

CONCLUSION

My family was not consulted when I began this journey of purpose. I probably should have talked to them, but it never occurred to me to consider the implications of praying this prayer: *"God, use me and our family to change the world—one individual at a time."*

I loved and love being a wife, and I loved and love being a mom of boys. I would give my life, my time, and my last dime to the men in my life. My longing to matter does not diminish these roles. I believe I am a better wife and mother because of this journey.

Since this writing, there have been over fifty girls who have called Courage House home and have called me Mom. Each is my daughter. Some are from here in the United States and some are from Tanzania, Africa. But sadly, because of a lack of space, we say no to more girls than we are able to help.

When each girl arrives at Courage House, I tell them the story I have told you through the pages of this book. They are also told that before time began they were created on purpose for a purpose; that God imagined them, planned them, and that He has something for them to do that only they can do; and that if they do not do it, it will never be done.

I tell each of them that although I cannot wipe away or even begin to explain the *why* of their past, I do promise them that we will walk with them into their future. I promise each child we will be there when the nightmares and flashbacks come. We will love them until they learn to love themselves. We will call them family. They will always have a home. And for those who have had to go … we pray that they will come back home.

Get up! Be bright! Stop playing small, for I have covered you with the bright light of my love, and my splendor shoots forth light beams from you and upon you. Though the world is a dark place, you bring the brightness of my love. I have made you to be bright so others will be drawn to you. My glory is literally on you. Stand. Rise. Be seen. Do not shrink from your destiny. You reflect my heart. Do not fear the darkness; it should fear you.

From the one who made you.

Go now. Have the courage to be you.

AUTHOR BIO

Jenny Williamson is the founder and CEO of Courage Worldwide, an international non-profit organization that builds homes for children rescued out of sex trafficking around the world. With Courage Houses successfully open in Northern California and Tanzania, Africa, Jenny works tirelessly to see rescued children fully restored so they can then hear the life-altering truth that they too were created on purpose for a purpose. Courage Houses are places where they can discover their true identity and fulfill their destiny.

For her efforts and impact in the community, Jenny was awarded the FBI Director's 2010 Community Leadership Award; the 2011 Community Spirit Award by Sacramento's District Attorney, Jan Scully; the 2012 William Jessup University's prestigious Community Impact Award; and she was invited to be part of the California Attorney General's Working Group on human trafficking. She was also part of Shared Hope International's Practitioners Working Group for their 2012 National Colloquium meeting in Washington, D.C. and is a member of Abolition International Shelter Association's advisory board. She is also the 2014 receipant of the prestigious Loreal Women of Worth Award.

As a professionally trained life coach and results-driven business leader, Jenny is known for her contagious energy, her motivational speeches, and her passion to change the world. She is an international speaker and has a passion to courageously be and do all God created her for—nothing more—and absolutely refuses to settle for less and encourages everyone she meets to do the same.

She and her family live in Northern California, where she also acts as chief financial officer of their family business. To book Jenny to speak at your next event, complete the speaker request form at jennytwilliamson.com. You can also follow Jenny on Facebook, Twitter, or Instagram.

For more information on the organization Jenny founded, or to be one of the million somebodies who are going to build one thousand homes in one hundred countries in ten years so hundreds of thousands of children can be rescued from the evil of sex trafficking, go to courageworldwide.org.